The Parents with Teenagers Handbook

Practical advice for Parents

ISBN   978-1-4717-8175-9
Copyright © 2012 Damon Bachegalup All rights reserved.
(Standard Copyright Licence)
First Edition
Publisher Damon Bachegalup

Acknowledgements

All of this would not have been possible without the love, help, support, guidance and proof reading skills of my wife (the love of my life) Erika

Contents

Foreword

If you are reading this book then it is safe to assume that you are already experiencing some sort of problems in relating to your young person. After writing my first book I was asked by parents to write a more in-depth handbook covering more teen life topic.

So, the main reasons for writing this book is to share my learned skills, my techniques and my ways in relating to young people with a straight and no nonsense approach which have benefited me in my different roles in life of being an Adult, a father, and a parent/step parent, a Counsellor, a Mentor and a Mediator.

It has worked both with my own children (who are now adults themselves), with friends children and other young people who have been through my Troubled Teen Therapy Programme at Teenbratcampuk.

As we know, children do not come with an instruction manual which can be used to refer to from time to time and at times of challenging behaviour from the young person. For the purpose of this book I will refer to the young people/person from now on as teenagers.

After identifying a lack of help and support in the UK for parents with troubled teens. He had to think outside the box and adapted the techniques of the standard counselling protocol to develop a more flexible and creative approach, being as flexible as is necessary for each young person.

Regardless of the challenges, I have been able to use my techniques to successfully work with a range of difficulties and issues with young people. Teenbratcampuk private and exclusive programmes are run by me I am one of the UK's leading professional Teenage Behaviourists BA (Hons)

DipCoun's. MBACP. CCYP. AIP. My goal is to help families to find solutions to the struggles they face at home with their troubled teen.

I have over 11 years experience of working with hard to engage teenagers as both a Behavioural Therapist and as a Mediator. I believe that my own life experiences are just as important as my professional and academic training in relating to young people. I am Dyslexic and left school at 15 without any qualifications. I am a counsellor/psychotherapist and have my own private practice. I am an Integrative Practitioner which means that I blend different methods of counselling according to the individual young persons needs and I have many years of experience working with young people and adults.

I will refer to the place where the teenager lives as "the family". I know the family may or may not be the traditional 'normal' family and there may be step-parents, Parents, foster carers, adopted parents, same sex parents and any of all the different combinations that we have in today society. As Trisha Goddard says 'the only thing that is 'normal' is a programme on a washing machine'.

However, I would like to state that the physical and biological make up of any family is in NO way a reason or excuse for a teenagers to behave in away that results in conflict, fear, violence, rudeness or generally being a pain in the backside at this time.

Chapter 1

Automatic Behavioural Mind.

When we deal with our teens we go into what I like to term as
"Automatic Behavioural Mind".
To illustrate this I will use an incident that most of us have
been through
Stage 1-
When we get into our car and turn the ignition key to the start
position, the engine turns but does not fire up, we turn the key
back to the off position wait a moment look around at the dash
board turn the radio off, check the lights are off, check the
indicator then turn the key to the on position again the engine
turns but still does not start.
Stage 2-
At this point we get out of the car, open the bonnet, look
around in the engine bay and then we will touch and jiggle the
battery leads, touch some of other wires we can see (even of
we aren't sure what they are for) and then tap on the top off
the engine. We then we get back in the car turn the key the
engine turns but still doss not start so we get back out of the
car and guess what I'm going to say next ! We go round to the
engine bay again and yes you know what I am going to say
next, we repeat what we have already done.
Stage 3-
 This time we touch and jiggle the wires more vigorously and
may even check other things apart from the engine like
checking the oil and water?? We will repeat these One, Two,
Three, Four or even more times.

So what have we learned? Well we know that touching the
wires did not work the first or second time but we feel and
believe that if we carry on touching them again and again and

pushing harder it will work. The fact is that it has not worked. At this point it is interesting to note that it is usually the male that is more likely to continue to repeat stage's one, two and there over and over saying 'well it worked last time I did it". The fact is that 'it is not working NOW'!! A female is more likely to stop after the 3rd time and then think   "I know I'll phone the breakdown company".

I know that as parents/adults we tend to continue to carry on doing the same things over and over that we have learned from our past even when we have the very facts and evidence that now it is no longer working and especially when it may have worked in the past or with other children at times in the family.

Chapter 2

Chalk and Cheese

All children and young people are different and react to life in different ways. At some stages, particularly pre-school and teenage years, children can find it hard to control emotions. This is a normal part of their development as they learn to cope with life and realise they can't have everything their own way.

Children also go through stages as their brains develop which I will look at later in the book and they try out different emotions and ways of reacting to the world. It's normal for younger children to have fears (for example, of ghosts or monsters or dogs), as they become aware there are dangers in the wider world around them and they learn to distinguish between reality and fiction. Many children develop patterns of behaviour to comfort themselves if they feel anxious, such as thumb sucking or wanting to do the same things at the same time every day.

As they get towards puberty, children can become more defiant as they start to be independent and separate psychologically from their parents and carer's and when the teen years begin, many young people become moody, angry or tearful and battles with parents can become a daily occurrence.

Personality plays a part too – some children are naturally more anxious than others and some express themselves physically or are very emotional while others are more reserved.

But if your child's behaviour has changed recently, or you have started worrying about it and are not sure if what they are going through is normal or not, it's worth thinking about the following:

Is the behaviour out of character for your child, or does it fit in with their general way of dealing with things?

Has the change been very sudden or have things been changing for a while?

Is there anything obvious that might have upset or unsettled them? For example, moving house or school, divorce and separation bereavement, friendship problems, illness.

Is the behaviour having a negative effect on their daily life, for example, stopping them attending school or getting their schoolwork done; affecting friendships or family relationships; getting in the way of hobbies or activities; affecting their eating or sleeping?

Is anyone else worried about their behaviour? e.g. other family members, teachers, friends.

Has your child said they think there is a problem or that they are worried?

There are no right answers, but these questions might help you think about what has been going on and whether it is normal for your child.

Interest and Curiosity in Life

Children have an interest and curiosity in life in general, and tend to do well at school. They have a varied and secure social life and an ability to communicate at all levels, whilst also being very aware of social and behavioural boundaries and the consequences of their actions.

All of a sudden your tiny, helpless and entirely dependent bundle of joy will start to grow up, do lots of things for themselves and gradually need you less and less.

This is what positive, effective and well balanced parenting is all about and if your child is independent, assertive, self confident and well balanced then you have done a pretty good job!

However, children develop their independence at very different stages and sometimes girls appear to be more independent than boys at an early age. The oldest child in a family may well become independent quicker than his or her younger brothers and sisters do, and some children may struggle with the whole concept of being self sufficient until they are considerably older than their peers.

All Children Are Different

Children all begin to gain their independence at different stages and find some parts of growing up easier than others. The key to continuing your positive parenting is to accept that all children are different and need different levels of support and guidance as they start to grow up.

One of the best things that any parents can do for their growing child is to equip them with the life tools they need in order to become more independent. You may feel that you want to keep your children as babies forever because this is how we can protect them and keep them from harmful influences.

Letting Go

However hard letting go of your child's childhood may seem, you have to think of them and how they are going to develop into a well balanced individual. You may feel that your role as a parent is not important anymore and that you are really not needed.

This is simply not the case at all, you will simply find that your role is changing and developing into something different just like your child is.

Equipping Your Child for Life

By ensuring that your child continues to feel safe, secure and loved by you, you will enable them to start becoming more independent, and this will actually make your life easier eventually!

Independence begins with small things such as a child being able to go to the toilet unaided, managing to pour their own drinks and put on their own coat. These development then progresses to getting themselves dressed in the morning and even getting their own breakfast-and this will happen sooner than you think!

Independence is also about children being able to make their own decisions and choices and by teaching them how to be confident and secure, your parenting skills will really come into play. You will find that the way you encourage your child to do things for themselves will help them enormously both at school and beyond. They will grow into confident young people who are able to help themselves to make decisions and find their way through life without too many problems.

As parents you will always have an important role to play in your child's life and they will always need your help, love and support and guidance-whatever their age and stage of their development.

All parents want their children to grow up to be resourceful, independent and well balanced young people, who enjoy their lives and feel secure and loved.

This process begins from an early age when we do simple things like encourage our children to dress themselves, bath themselves and cope on their own at school. As well as encouraging independence, parents should also be thinking about encouraging their children to be resourceful.

Children Have Their Own Ideas

It is very easy to spoon feed our children for too long; giving them everything they could possibly need or want in any situation. It is far better to allow our children to make discoveries for themselves, and encourage them to find ways to do things and keep themselves occupied and entertained.

Children find great delight in making their own choices and discoveries, and this starts from any early age with the simplest of things such as finding out what happens when you mix two paint colours together, right up to making choices about how to do their homework, make friends and find a hobby that they enjoy.

Give Your Children Freedom

Children need boundaries and guidelines, and although overly permissive parenting has become increasingly popular in recent times, allowing your child to have absolute freedom does not always encourage resourcefulness. In fact it can have quite the opposite affect.

Children who are given access to everything are often those who are over indulged and don't actually have to think for themselves very much at all. Because their parents have simply allowed them the ultimate freedom to do and behave as they wish, without clearly defined boundaries they will not necessarily become truly resourceful.

Guidance Is Key

Instead, make suggestions to your children about things, give them the tools in terms of confidence and self esteem to make informed choices and decisions, and then allow them the freedom to find solutions. This way they draw on their own, true resources while acknowledging that there are boundaries and guidelines for life, and why they are so important.

Children need help and guidance at every stage of their development, and need to understand why boundaries are needed while at the same time having confidence instilled in them that allows them to find solutions to problems, and ways to occupy, entertain and amuse themselves.

Simple acts like encouraging your child to order their own food in a restaurant, paying for their own sweets and comics in a shop, asking the way to somewhere, finding out about opening times of the cinema or just finding the best way to get

A to fit into B, are all methods that are simple but will really help your child to develop their resourcefulness and independence from an early age.

Having a resourceful child who can call on their own knowledge and expertise to problem solve and make informed choices and decisions, also makes your life as a parent much easier. It means that you know your child can cope in certain situations, and with their knowledge and understanding of the importance of boundaries will find a way through most situations independently.

Teenage rebellion is a part of growing up, of establishing independence and signalling that your teenager isn't a child any more. To a greater or lesser degree everyone has done it. It maybe that one day the child you thought of as sweet comes home looking punk or Goth and all you can do is stare in shock when they ask what you think. It's their rebellion, or at least one facet of it. It could be the same with a change in musical tastes, and behaviour.

Chapter 3

Teenager (noun)

Stereotypical view of the teenager
Kevin the teenager first appeared in the "Little Brother"
sketches of Harry Enfield's Television Programme as an
annoyingly energetic boy who constantly vexed his older
brother with his irritating catchphrases and habit of bursting
into his room when he was with a girl.

In the first episode of Harry Enfield and Chums, Kevin, now
without his older brother, reached his thirteenth birthday. The
sketch showed his parents watching in horror as Kevin lost his
sense of dress, courtesy and posture as the clock struck
midnight on the day of his thirteenth birthday, thus becoming
Kevin the Teenager, one of the most memorable of Enfield's
comic creations.

Wearing a baseball cap the wrong way round and with his red
hair flopping over his face, Kevin is rude to his despairing
parents, frequently shouting "I hate you, I wish I'd never been
born!" at them, and insisting that everything is "so unfair!". In
one sketch, when his father asks him to wash his car, Kevin
ends up taking the entire day to complete the task due to his
inability to get out of bed before noon and an apparent allergy
to work, and in another sketch, though wide awake, he made
the most primitive of attempts at tidying his room when
required to do so. The character is also heavily dictated by
peer pressure, and was seen in various other sketches trying to
sound like Ail G, or people in Oasis.

His best friend is another teenaged boy named Perry (played
by the actress Kathy Burke, and based on an early character
Burke portrayed on various Channel 4 shows). They starred in
a 2000 feature film, Kevin & Perry Go Large.

The sketches suggest that teenage boys are always very polite
to all parents except their own. Kevin and Perry heap

immense amounts of abuse on their own respective parents (though Perry shouts at his down the phone rather than face to face) yet are very polite to each other's parents. In one sketch, Kevin's plans to host a party go wrong and end with the house being trashed. Despite his frequent declarations of hatred towards his parents, Kevin ends up crying whilst his long-suffering mother gives him a much needed hug.

Aside from playing video games, Kevin's one aim in life is to lose his virginity, or at least to prove that he has a girlfriend. From boasting about the (imagined) joys of sex to placing the nozzle of a vacuum cleaner to his neck to look as though he has received a love bite, he is determined to prove that he has "done it". He eventually does lose his virginity in one sketch during a drunken party. The following morning, he wakes up transformed into a nice, polite and helpful young man, this however does not last.

Due to Kevin and the other characters in *Harry Enfield and Chums'* getting positive feedback and statements of the truth behind the writers' observations, the term "Kevin the Teenager" (often shortened to simply a "Kevin"), has entered British vernacular to describe any adolescent who is bad-tempered or rebellious ("He's a right Kevin!") It can even be applied to female adolescents.

Many parents will now be saying "yes that sounds like my teen what went wrong"? Whether you gave birth to or adopted your child, parents rarely consider the possibility that their little bundle of joy they brought into their lives may someday turn into a "Kevin" or a Vicky Pollard.

Teenager (noun)

1) A mammal found extensively throughout the planet, often clustered in groups in front of television sets and computer games. Thought to be a member of Homo Sapiens due to physical similarities, though social and emotional behaviour

leads many researchers to consider Teenagers to be a completely different species altogether. Very, very territorial.

Teenagers are extraordinarily social animals, seeking contact with their peer groups to such a great extent they will forgo family, chores, sleep, food, and responsibility. The males of the species forage for food constantly and can consume three times their weight every day. When in full plumage, the males are usually drab, marked by loose fitting garments which slide off their backsides and look ridiculous therefore making it impossible to walk correctly.

The females, on the other hand, sport striking colours under their eyes, over the eyes, throughout their hair, and on the tips of their fingers and toes. Females often attract males by wearing garments to accentuate chest development. Males indicate their approval by staring at the display. The call of the female is complex and shrill: "Like, OMG, OMG, Whatever" Males are less vocal, signalling to other males with a salutatory "Yo. Yo. Yo. S'up? S'up? S'up ?, Whatever"

Teenagers line their nests with discarded undergarments, Clothes, discarded plates of food and cups that once held a soft drink but have now morphed into something strange, green and furry. The females hold telephone receivers to their ears for an average of six hours a day. When challenged for possession, they snarl and warn intruders, "I'm doing my HOMEWORK, My HOMEWORK, My HOMEWORK". The males lie immobile for hours at a time, conserving energy and listening to violent electronic signals from radios. Male Teenagers concentrate on important information by rolling their eyes, shrugging, kicking dirt, tutting and sighing. Females burst into tears and slam doors. Both may shout "I HATE YOU" at various stages.

Many Homo Sapiens families have a host-to-parasite relationship with one or more than one Teenager. These host families often develop a resistance to the parasite, rejecting them some time in their eighteenth year of life. Often, though, this rejection is merely theoretical, with the Teenager continuing to live off of the host Homo Sapiens family for many years afterward, often at great sacrifice.

In adults, various parts of the brain work together to evaluate choices, make decisions and act accordingly in each situation. The teenage brain doesn't appear to work like this. For comparison's sake, think of the teenage brain as an entertainment centre that hasn't been fully hooked up. There are loose wires, so that the speaker system isn't working with the DVD player, which in turn hasn't been formatted to work with the television yet. And to top it all off, the remote control hasn't even arrived, never mind the batteries!

Chapter 4

History of the Teenager

In 1900 teenagers did not exist. There were young people in their teens, but there was no culture or institution that united them or fostered peer group development on a societal scale. While some worked at home, on family farms, or in factories or offices, others attended school. Still more married or prepared for marriage. One hundred years later, in 2000, teenagers were impossible to avoid. There were more teens than ever before and their cultural presence was undeniable. They existed not only as high school students, but as highly sought consumers, carefully watched as trendsetters in FASHION, music, and MOVIES.

In the public imagination teenagers first appeared after World War II, complete with distinctive dress, habits, and culture. The period before 1950, however, proved crucial for the formation of teenagers in the UK. After 1900 reformers, educators, and legislators began to separate teens from adults and children. The legal system created JUVENILE COURTS. The governments legislated minimum age requirements for sexual consent, marriage, school attendance, and work, and later for voting, driving, and drinking alcohol. Often inconsistent, some legislation further divided teens by gender. Girls, for example, could marry younger than boys, but could not legally consent to sexual activity until later.

The dramatic rise in Secondary School attendance was the single most important factor in creating teenage culture. High school, based on biological age, reshaped the experiences of thirteen- to eighteen-year-olds. Between 1910 and 1930, enrolment in secondary schools increased almost 400 percent. The proportion of fourteen- to-seventeen-year olds in high school increased from 10.6 percent in 1901 to 51.1 percent in 1930 and 71.3 percent in 1940. Graduation rates remained low but still rose from 29.0 percent in 1930 to 50.8 percent in 1940. As enrolment grew, the student body changed. No longer an elite institution, students increasingly came from all socioeconomic, ethnic, and racial groups. Educators redesigned rapidly expanding schools to foster responsible citizens, promote social order, and, during the Depression, to keep teens out of the labour market. High schools also promoted unsupervised peer interaction.

During the 1920s, 1930s, and 1940s, some manufacturers, marketers, and retailers also began to recognise high schoolers, especially girls, as consumers with purchasing power and style preferences. Simultaneously, teenagers began to develop a "teenage" identity and recognize their collective strength. Social scientists and parents also engaged in the extensive dialogue over the nature of ADOLESCENCE, high school, and the growing concept *teenager*. Scholarly work, popular advice, and parental strategies emerged alongside the developing high school culture and teen CONSUMER CULTURE. Gendered differences remained–literature on boys emphasized education, work, and rebellion, whereas literature on girls addressed behaviour, appearance, and relationships. Media also played an important role, often defining *teenager* as female. Media served to promote teenage trends by offering publicity and a national means for reaching other teens. But by the early 1940s, the BOBBY SOXER stereotype dominated, which negatively portrayed teenage girls as mindless worshipers of celebrities and adolescents fads.

Recognised as separate from the adolescent, the teenager more closely related to high school culture. Use of the words *teen, teener, teen-age,* and even *teenager* first appeared in the 1920s and 1930s. They referred to thirteen- to eighteen-year-olds, increasingly conceptualized as a distinct cohort in media, popular literature, and advertisements. As teenage culture emerged, teens used mass-produced commodities to imitate adults, but they also used them to create fads and to define themselves as teenagers.

Chapter 5

The Teenage Brain

The brain's remote control is the **prefrontal cortex**, a section of the brain that weighs outcomes, forms judgments and controls impulses and emotions. This section of the brain also helps people to understand one another. If you were to walk into a sports bar full of Manchester United fans wearing a Manchester City Top, your prefrontal cortex would immediately begin firing in warning; those teams are bitter enemies, and it might serve you to change your behaviour (and your clothes). The prefrontal cortex communicates with the other sections of the brain through connections called **synapses**. These are like the wires of the entertainment system.

What scientists have found is that teenagers experience a wealth of growth in synapses during adolescence. But if you've ever hooked up an entertainment center, you know that more wires mean more problems. You tend to keep the components you use the most, while getting rid of something superfluous, like an out-of-date laserdisc player. The brain works the same way, because it starts pruning away the synapses that it doesn't need in order to make the remaining ones much more efficient in communicating. In teenagers, it seems that this process starts in the back of the brain and moves forward, so that the prefrontal cortex, that vital center of control, is the last to be trimmed. As the connections are trimmed down, an insulating substance called **myelin** coats the synapses to protect them.

As such, the prefrontal cortex is a little immature in teenagers as compared to adults; it may not fully develop until your mid-20s. And if you don't have a remote control to call the shots in the brain, using the other brain structures can become more difficult. Imaging studies have shown that most of the mental energy that teenagers use in making decisions is located in the back of the brain, whereas adults do most of their processing in the frontal lobe [source: Wallis]. When teenagers do use the frontal lobe, it seems they overdo it, calling upon much more of the brain to get the job done than adults would [source: Powell]. And because adults have already refined those communicating synapses, they can make decisions more quickly.

Adult brains are also better wired to notice errors in decision-making. While adults performed tasks that required the quick response of pushing buttons, their brains sent out a signal when a hasty mistake was made. Before 80 milliseconds had passed, adult brains had noticed the blunder, but teenage brains didn't notice any slip-up.

An area of the teenager's brain that is fairly well-developed early on, though, is the **nucleus accumbens**, or the area of the brain that seeks pleasure and reward. In imaging studies that compared brain activity when the subject received a small, medium or large reward, teenagers exhibited exaggerated responses to medium and large rewards compared to children and adults [source: Powell]. When presented with a small reward, the teenagers' brains hardly fired at all in comparison to adults and children.

So what does it mean to have an undeveloped prefrontal cortex in conjunction with a strong desire for reward? As it happens, this combination could explain a lot of stereotypical teenage behavior.

Setting the Stage--Adolescence
The limitations of the "teen brain" has been well publicized in the mass media, helping parents, teachers, and others understand why it may be difficult for teens to meet our expectations and demands for managing emotions, handling

risks, responding to relationships, and engaging in complex school work or employment. In early- and mid-adolescence, the brain undergoes considerable growth and pruning, moving generally from back to front areas of the cerebral cortex.

Changes in Young Adulthood

At the same time that young adults are experiencing new levels of sophistication in thinking and emotional regulation, their brains are undergoing changes in precisely the areas associated with these functions. While it is not possible to determine cause-and-effect, brain and behaviour are changing in parallel.

Prefrontal cortex: The most widely studied changes in young adulthood are in the prefrontal cortex, the area behind the forehead associated with planning, problem-solving, and related tasks. At least two things affect the efficiency in its functioning:

myelination: the nerve fibres' are more extensively covered with myelin, a substance that insulates them so that signals can be transmitted more efficiently, and

synaptic pruning: the "briar patch" of connections resulting from nerve growth are pruned back, allowing the remaining ones to transmit signals more efficiently.

Connections among regions:

At the same time, the prefrontal cortex communicates more fully and effectively with other parts of the brain, including those that are particularly associated with emotion and impulses, so that all areas of the brain can be better involved in planning and problem-solving.

"Executive suite":

The cluster of functions that centre in the prefrontal cortex is sometimes called the "executive suite," including calibration of risk and reward, problem-solving, prioritizing, thinking ahead, self-evaluation, long-term planning, and regulation of emotion. (See Merlin Donald, Daniel Keating, and others in

References.) It is not that these tasks cannot be done before young adulthood, but rather that it takes less effort, and hence is more likely to happen.

20s and beyond

According to recent findings, the human brain does not reach full maturity until at least the mid-20s. (See J. Giedd in References.) The specific changes that follow young adulthood are not yet well studied, but it is known that they involve increased myelination and continued adding and pruning of neurons. As a number of researchers have put it, "the rental car companies have it right." The brain isn't fully mature at 16, when we are allowed to drive, or at 18, when we are allowed to vote, or at 21, when we are allowed to drink, but closer to 25, when we are allowed to rent a car.

Chapter 6

Teenage Growth & Development: 11-14 Years

Quick Facts
The physical changes that take place during puberty are
caused by hormones.
A girl will usually get her first period around the same age
that her mother did.
Because teens want to fit in, most choose friends whose
interests, activities, and values are similar to their own.
Talking on the phone is one way teens develop their social
skills.
Physical changes (Puberty)
For girls, puberty begins around 10 or 11 years of age and
ends around age 16. Boys enter puberty later than girls-
usually around 12 years of age-and it lasts until around age 16
or 17. Girls and boys usually begin puberty around the same
time their mothers and fathers did. Talk with your child about
the following physical changes that will happen during
puberty. The changes are listed in the order in which they
generally occur.

Girls
body fat increases
breasts begin to enlarge
pubic hair grows
height and weight increase
first menstrual period occurs
hips widen
underarm hair grows
skin and hair become more oily
pimples may appear
Boys
scrotum becomes darker

testicles grow larger
penis grows longer and fuller
pubic hair grows
breasts can get "lumps" and become tender
height and weight increase
muscles develop
wet dreams occur
voice cracks and gets deeper
skin and hair become more oily
pimples may appear
underarm and facial hair grow
Intellectual development

Most 11- to 14-year-olds are still concrete thinkers-they
perceive things as good or bad, right or wrong. This is normal.
They are just beginning to imagine possibilities, recognize
consequences of their actions, and anticipate what others are
thinking.
Youth begin to question family and school rules and challenge
their parents.
Preteens and teens tend to believe that bad things won't
happen to them. This helps explain why they are risk-takers.
For example, a young girl may believe she can smoke
cigarettes without becoming addicted.
Preteens and teens believe they are the center of attention.
This explains why they are painfully self-conscious--a tiny
pimple may seem like the end of the world.
Social and emotional development
Preteens and teens begin to spend more time with peers and
less time with family.
Preteens and teens begin to form their identity by exploring
different clothes, hairstyles, friends, music, and hobbies.
Moodiness is common as youth struggle to search for an
identity.

Preteens and teens push limits that adults put on them to assert their independence.

Preteens and teens have mixed feelings about "breaking away" from parents. One day your daughter may want nothing to do with you, the next she is constantly at your side.

Troubled youth may act out (for example, get into physical fights, use alcohol or other drugs, skip school) to express emotional pain.

Tips for Parents

Preteens and teens are sometimes embarrassed by their changing bodies and concerned that they are not developing at the same rate as their friends. Reassure your child that young people grow and develop at their own pace and that the changes are normal.

Do not tease your child about pubertal changes.

Explain the importance of good personal hygiene. Active sweat glands call for regular bathing and deodorant. For healthy teeth, everyone should brush twice a day with a fluoride toothpaste and floss daily.

Set reasonable and appropriate limits. Preteens and teens want guidance.

When differences arise, listen to your child and try to understand his or her point of view.

Choose your battles! Hold your ground on important issues such as grades and drugs, and let go of smaller issues such as hairstyles and clothes. If it won't matter a year from now, is it worth arguing over?

Allow your preteen or teen to make more decisions as he or she proves the ability to use good judgment.

If your child is acting out, talk with him or her to get to the heart of the problem.

Get counseling for your child or the whole family if you believe it could help.

Talk with other parents about your concerns, their parenting experiences, setting limits, etc.

Teenage Growth & Development: 15-17 Years

Congratulations! You and your teen have made it through what is usually the most difficult period of adolescence -- 11 to 14 years. Mid-adolescence (15-17 years) is usually an easier time for teens and parents. But don't get too comfortable. New challenges will test your patience, understanding, and parenting skills.

Quick Facts

Most teens navigate the developmental tasks of adolescence successfully.

Teens ages 15-19 have much higher mortality rates than younger children.

The leading causes of death for teens are motor vehicle crashes, homicide, and suicide.

Physical growth

Girls have usually reached full physical development. Many teenage girls are concerned with the way they look and are dissatisfied with their bodies and their weight. Nearly half of all high school girls diet to lose weight. Boys are close to completing their physical growth. Around 15 or 16 years of age, boys' voices will lower and facial hair will appear. Boys may continue to gain height and muscle.

Intellectual characteristics

Teens are better able to solve problems, think about their future, appreciate opinions of others and understand the long-term effects of their decisions. However, teens tend to use these skills inconsistently; as a result, they sometimes do things without thinking first.

Teens' organizational skills improve. Many successfully juggle school, outside activities, and work.

In an attempt to answer the questions "Who am I?" and "What should I be?" teens listen to new music, try out clothing fashions, and begin to explore jobs, religion, political issues, and social causes.

Teens frequently question and challenge school and parental rules.

Social and emotional characteristics

Older teens are more self-assured and better able to resist peer pressure than younger teens.

Teens spend less time than they used to with their families. They prefer to spend more time with friends or alone.

Teens try to make close friends and may become part of a group based on interests or attributes (sports, arts, etc.).

Teens want control over more aspects of their life.

Teens are excited and at the same time overwhelmed by the possibilities for their future (college, work, or military).

Like adults, teens get depressed-sadness lasting more than 2 weeks, however, is not normal. Call your teen's health care provider if this happens.

Use of alcohol, tobacco, and other drugs is more common now than before.

Teens begin to have strong sexual urges, and many become sexually active.

Teens become more aware of their sexual orientation (homosexual, heterosexual, bisexual).

Tips for Parents

Breaking away from parents or guardians and wanting more privacy are normal parts of growing up-don't take it personally.

Although they won't admit it, teens still need parents to set limits. Rules and privileges (curfew, driving, dating, etc.) should be based on your teen's level of maturity, not age.

Negotiate rules with your teen. The more controlling you try to be, the more rebellious your teen is likely to become.

Discuss the consequences of breaking the rules and follow through with them if your teen misbehaves.

Teens will make mistakes and may lose your trust. It's important to give them another chance.

Express your values about school, work, alcohol and other drugs, and sex.

Encourage your teen to take aptitude and interest tests at school to identify future directions. Help your teen plan for his or her future after high school.

If your teen tells you that he or she is homosexual, he or she will need your love and support. You, in turn, may benefit from a support group for parents of gays and lesbians.

Know how to recognize the signs and symptoms of eating disorders and other mental health problems. Deal with any problem right away.

Talk with your teen about ways to handle pressure to drink, smoke, have sex, etc. Teach your teen how to say no and to suggest doing something different (safe). To feel comfortable talking openly with you, your teen needs to know that you will not punish him or her for being honest.

Social Development during the Teen Years
Adolescence is the period of developmental transition between childhood and adulthood. It involves changes in personality, as well as in physical, intellectual and social development. During this time of change, teens are faced with many issues and decisions. The following addresses some of the key issues that can have an impact on a teen's social development.

Self-esteem
Self-esteem is how you feel about yourself. The development of a positive self-image and a healthy self-esteem is very important for making a successful transition from child to adult. Here are some suggestions for helping to encourage positive self-esteem in your teen:

Give your child words of encouragement each day.

Remember to point out the things your child does right, not just the mistakes.

Be generous with praise.

Give constructive criticism, and avoid criticism that takes the form of ridicule or shame.

Teach your child about decision-making and make it a point to recognize when he or she has made a good decision.

Help your child learn to focus on his or her strengths by pointing out all of his or her talents and abilities.

Allow your teen to make mistakes. Overprotection or making decisions for teens can be perceived as a lack of faith in their abilities. This can make them feel less confident.

When disciplining your child, replace shame and punishment with positive reinforcement for good behaviour. Shame and punishment can make an adolescent feel worthless and inadequate.

Chapter 7

Peer pressure

As children grow, they begin to spend more time with their friends and less time with their parents. As a result, friends can influence a child's thinking and behaviour. This is the essence of peer pressure. Peer pressure can be a positive influence--for example, when it motivates your child to do well in school, or to become involved in sports or other activities. On the other hand, peer pressure can be a negative influence--for example, when it prompts your child to try smoking, drinking, using drugs, or to practice unsafe sex or other risky behaviours. Here are some tips to help minimize the negative influences of peer pressure and to maximize the positive:

Develop a close relationship with your child, and encourage open and honest communication. Children who have good relationships with their parents are more likely to seek a parent's advice about decisions or problems.

Help your child understand what peer pressure is. The child will be better able to resist negative influences if he or she understands what's happening and why.

Reinforce the values that are important to you and your family.

Nurture your teen's own abilities and self-esteem so that he or she is not as susceptible to the influences of others.

Teach your child how to be assertive, and praise assertive behaviour.

Give your teen breathing room. Don't expect him or her to do exactly as you say all of the time.

Try to avoid telling your child what to do; instead, listen closely and you may discover more about the issues influencing your child's behaviour.

Provide discipline. Your child needs to understand that there are consequences to negative behaviours.

Chapter 8

Tobacco, drugs and alcohol

Drug abuse is a serious problem that can lead to serious, even fatal, consequences. Research suggests that nearly 25 percent of adolescents (ages 12 to 17) have used drugs, with 16 to 18 as the peak age for drinking and drug abuse.

Teens whose parents regularly communicate with them about the dangers of drugs have a decreased risk of using tobacco, alcohol or other drugs. Following are some tips for addressing drugs, alcohol and tobacco use with your teen:

Set a good example. If you smoke, drink heavily or use drugs, you are teaching your child that these behaviours are acceptable.

Teach your child that drugs, tobacco and alcohol can harm their bodies, and that it's OK to say "no."

Teach your child how to avoid situations where others may be drinking, smoking or using drugs, and to choose friends who do not use these substances.

Know who your child's friends are, and don't allow your child to attend parties where there is no adult supervision.

Encourage your child to become involved in extra-curricular activities at school, a church youth group, or other programs that provide opportunities for teens to gather and socialise in a fun and safe environment.

Chapter 9

Teens and sex

Talking with your teenager is important to help him or her develop healthy attitudes toward sex and to learn responsible sexual behaviour. Openly discussing sex with your teen also enables you to provide accurate information. After all, teens will learn about sex somewhere. But what they learn might not be true, and might not reflect the personal and moral values and principles you want your children to follow. In addition, teens need to understand the possible consequences of being sexually active--including pregnancy and sexually transmitted diseases, as well as being emotionally hurt.
When you talk to your teen about sex, focus on the facts. Consider using the following list of topics as an outline:
Explanation of anatomy and reproduction in males and females
Sexual intercourse and pregnancy
Fertility and birth control
Other forms of sexual behaviour, including oral sex, masturbation and petting
Sexual orientation, including heterosexuality, homosexuality and bisexuality
The physical and emotional aspects of sex, including the differences between males and females
Self-image and peer pressure
Sexually transmitted diseases
Rape and date rape, including how being intoxicated (drunk or high), or accepting rides/going to private places with strangers or acquaintances puts you at risk
How choice of clothing and the way you present yourself sends messages to others about your interest in sexual behaviour (for example, tongue piercing, wearing low-cut clothing)

The UK has the highest rate of teen pregnancy in Europe. Politicians and experts keep debating the causes for it, and possible solutions, but the fact is that it's not decreasing.

It's a nightmare for every parent that their teen daughter will come home one day and say she's pregnant or that their son will tell them that his girlfriend is pregnant. A bad dream that happens to a lot of people.

But what do you do if it's your teen involved?

Girls

You have to understand that it's a huge step for your teen to tell you she's pregnant. She's probably agonised over it, and is expecting a firestorm to descend on her. Don't react that way. Be calm, be patient, and be understanding.

The first thing to do is confirm she's pregnant. Of course there are home pregnancy testing kits, but it's better to get her to the GP or to a local agency that specialises in services for young people. They can give confirmation of the pregnancy, and if your teen is pregnant, outline the options available to her.

There are three real options – keeping the baby, giving it up for adoption, or having an abortion. Your family might be one where abortion is not even a possibility for religious or other reasons, which narrows the choices.

Talk calmly and sensibly with your daughter. There's no point in berating her and making her feel a failure, she'll be in enough turmoil already. You have to work with her to come up with a plan of action that will work for you all.

Involve her boyfriend, since he's equally responsible for this, and his parents if at all possible. Talk to them separately, and see if together you can offer support to the couple.

If she wants to keep the child, your daughter can certainly continue at school until she gives birth, then take 18 weeks off before returning to finish her education, and many do follow that course. Some feel uncomfortable, and instead pursue home schooling or finish at a college, both of which are quite permissible. The Care to Learn programme can even help with childcare costs after she's given birth so she can afford to complete her education, as long as she's under the age of 20. If abortion or adoption is chosen, the young people's agency will be able to help with referrals. Bear in mind that with abortion, the sooner it's carried out, the safer the procedure. Above all, your daughter will need your support and your love, whichever choice she makes. If she keeps the baby, you'll almost certainly be helping with the childcare, so be prepared for that and discuss what and how much you're willing to do, emphasising that the main responsibility lies with her.

Boys

It's as hard for a boy's parents to hear that his girlfriend is pregnant as it is for the girl's parents to get the news. Again, you need to be calm, and talk to the girl's parents, work with them if at all possible, and not apportion any blame – it takes two to make a baby.

If the girl decides to keep the child, there's a lot you and your son can do in practical terms, with childcare, money, and making sure your son takes an active, ongoing role in the raising of his child. For boys there might be a tendency to run from the problem, but gently insist that your son does his share.

Whatever happens, don't reject your child – and your grandchild. People make mistakes, but sometimes they turn out to be the best things in the world.

Chapter 10

Puberty

It's the great divide between childhood and the teenage years, although, in fact, it continues through most of those teenage years. It's physical and emotional, and it can be scary for those going through it.

Your kids will have been prepared for it by lectures and films at school. But knowing what's going to happen, and having seen it in older siblings or friends doesn't really make it any easier for those in the middle of it. The body's changing in very visible ways, and there's no control over that. But with all the hormones racing around, kids are growing and changing mentally, too, and nothing anyone can say can prepare them for that.

As a parent, you're caught in the middle. You want to help, but in some ways you can't. However, there are things that you can do.

The Physical Changes

These days puberty begins at a younger age and many kids will experience a lot of it even before the teenage years. For girls the breasts begin to grow, the body shape starts to change and menstruation commences. For boys it's hair growth, a rapid rise in height and the voice breaking.

As a parent, you see all this starting to happen. That's the time to sit down with your teen and go over what will change and how. Yes, they'll have heard it all in school already, but it's different when they start to feel it, and home is the place where they feel secure. Remember, they're not in control of any of this, and they're certainly not emotionally developed enough to handle it. You can be their rock, assure them that it's perfectly normal, that they're not turning into freaks and help them be ready for what lies ahead.

That's especially important for girls, since there's really no telling when menstruation will start. They'll be caught unawares, but if they know exactly what to expect and what to do there'll be far less of a sense of panic.

The more you can do to help your kids prepare for all this, the easier a time they'll have, and approach the inevitable changes with more confidence. You'll see your babies rocket up and gradually change into adults before your eyes. For them it can be a remarkable process, for you it can be sad, all a part of them growing up and letting go. But it's life, and there's nothing to be done about it except love them and help them. By the time teens are around 14, most of the major physical changes will have happened. But the process hasn't ended. They'll continue to grow, and in the case of boys fill out much more, until their late teens, so be prepared!

Emotional Changes

As if the physical growth and changes weren't quite enough, there's a strong emotional component, too, the one that leads to the moodiness of teens. In some ways that can be much harder for parents.

The best thing you can do is offer your support, be available to talk and, if asked, give your advice. However hard the time is for you (and some teens can make it very tough indeed), remember that it's even harder for your teens.

Puberty is such a confusing, troubling time for teens. Be patient, and give them positive comments about their appearance and looks, since they'll need it more than ever before.

Menstruation can be a very scary thing for young teens. If they know about it at all they likely know only that it involves blood and pain, and for teens who have not had their first period this can seem like an intensely personal, frighteningly unique and potentially embarrassing event. Parents of teens should strive to discuss menstruation before a girl's first menstrual period, and to do so in private, with "props" and in a positive light which will help impart information without irrational fear.

Discussing In Private
Regardless of the fact that menstruation is a totally natural process, very few teens want to discuss it in public the way they might mention an ear infection or how long their hair grows. Menstruation involves the reproductive system so from the start it is a more personal topic that deserves the respect of privacy. Generally mothers talk to their daughters about menstruation, and doing so during a girls-only dinner or "girls' night in" can help to make it a special chat. Teens may not particularly want to have this conversation in public, such as at a restaurant where others could overhear, so arranging to talk in the privacy of your own home is probably best. Also, make sure that you do truly talk and don't fall into lecture mode. Allow your teen to ask questions and remind her that you are available any time she has another question or concern.

Discussing With "Props"
If a teen has not yet had her first menstrual period it can be hard for her to understand exactly what menstruation is all about. For example, she may know that there will likely be "pain" associated, but she will not yet understand how severe, when it will strike, how long it will last, what she can do to relieve it or how it will affect her regular schedule. Bringing along concrete items such as tampons and sanitary napkins will at least allow her to interact with these objects before she needs them. In fact, giving her a box of each to have on hand

for when she does get her period may help her feel more in control.

Discussing In a Positive Light
It can be very easy to fall back on negative depictions of menstruation: PMT, cramps and bleeding are not necessarily fun events. However, try to impart to your teen that menstruation is a truly positive cycle. It not only means that a young woman is maturing, but it is related to giving life. Discuss with your teen what menstruation means (that a young woman can now become pregnant) and your own thoughts on teen sex, sexuality and pregnancy. This may become a perfect springboard for a discussion of birth control and house rules regarding romantic relationships. The same can be said for the opposite – while you are discussing sex or birth control you can segue into a discussion of menstruation. This may be particularly appealing if you are speaking with a boy and wouldn't otherwise bring up menstruation on its own. Menstruation can be wondrous and worrying at the same time, so arming teens with information before they need it should help keep everyone calm. And try not to wait for your teen to come to you – be bold and broach the subject on your own.

Chapter 11

Safe Sex

Though the term "safe sex" floats around freely, the only truly safe sex is no sex at all. Any time someone engages in sexual activities there can be a risk of contracting a sexually transmitted infection (STI) or getting pregnant. Using contraception, otherwise known as birth control can lower some of these risks. In order for teens to avoid unintended consequences of sexual activity they need to know the facts about keeping themselves safe. Discussing birth control with your teen is a great way to both share information and your own views of sexual activity and sexual health.

Discussing Teen Sexuality

Teens hate lectures, and they often hate soul-searching conversations with their parents almost as much. However parents should persist if they are to have an open, honest conversation about teen sexual health. Before discussing methods of safer sex parents should discuss sex and sexuality. "Sexuality" is a term often used to describe only an individual's sexual orientation but it actually encompasses all of the sexual thoughts, feelings, behaviours, preferences and development of an individual. While there's probably no need to go into detail about personal experiences, letting your teen know your views on teen sex is an important part of helping them navigate their own sexuality.

Discussing Contraceptive Options

There are many methods of contraception available today, including the birth control pill, the birth control patch, condoms, contraceptive implants, contraceptive injections, intra-uterine devices and diaphragms. The rhythm method and withdrawal are also sometimes considered types of contraception. As you discuss each type of birth control with your teen, be sure to remind him or her that there is no option that is 100% effective 100% of the time. Also be sure that your teen understands that only condoms work to prevent both pregnancy and STIs, so they should be worn at all times during sexual activities.

Discussing Abortion

Abortion is a divisive issue and some people do see it as a method of birth control. Tell your teen frankly what you think of abortion, but remember that if a teen does find him or herself dealing with an unplanned pregnancy that (s)he will likely be scared and confused - the exact time that (s)he could use guidance. If possible, stress that you would like to be there for your teen if (s)he finds him or herself in such a situation. Sometimes teens need this "permission" before truly believing that you will want to help them.

Further Information on Contraception

If you feel that your teen would benefit from further, professional information about contraception then there are a variety of places that you can send them. Your GP may be able to provide information about birth control and your local family planning clinic can be found at the fpa (formerly the Family Planning Association) (www.fpa.org.uk). Brooks Advisory Clinics (www.brook.org.uk) also offer information on sexual health and contraception to teens. You may consider telling your teen that you would be happy to take them for a consultation, or that you are fine with them going on there own. Whatever your thoughts, be sure to share them with your teen so that there is no confusion later.

Birth control can be a tough topic for parents and teens to discuss, but it is a relevant issue regarding teen health and safety. If and when you do decide to speak to your teen about contraception, be sure to bring it up in the wider context of teen sexuality and offer information on different birth control options, your opinions on abortion and where teens can find further information on birth control as needed.

Many parents understand the importance of discussing safer sex and sexual health with their teens, but far fewer consider discussing sexuality with their teens. Perhaps this is because parents think there is no need, or because they are unwilling to discuss anything beyond what is absolutely necessary to keep their child healthy and safe. Whatever the case, teen sexuality is an important topic and one that parents should consider talking about with their teens.

Teen Sexuality
"Sexuality" is a term often used to describe only an individual's sexual orientation but it also includes much more. Sexuality encompasses all of the sexual thoughts, feelings, behaviours, preferences and development of an individual. Obviously sexuality is a very private matter, one that rarely requires justification or defence to others. However, parents should consider bringing up the topic of teen sexuality so that their children understand that it is not a topic that is off-limits, and in fact is one that their parents are happy to discuss.

Private Discussions
Very few people would feel comfortable discussing their sexuality in front of a large group, so don't expect this of your teen. If you would like to talk about sexuality, do so in a private setting and be prepared to discuss topics that you may never have even heard mentioned in front of your teen before. There will no doubt be a steep learning curve to these discussions in terms of finding out what you are comfortable with, what your teen is comfortable with, what you can joke about and what you can not abide talking about, but in order to have an open and honest relationship with your child you'll need to confront this challenge head-on.

Remain Open

Not only is it imperative to remain open during discussions of sexuality, but it is important to remain open after they close as well. Parents who abruptly end a conversation send the signal that they are uncomfortable and therefore unwilling to talk about this subject matter. However, parents who do their best to answer questions, talk about sensitive topics and encourage their children to come to them when they have new thoughts or questions send the signal that not only are they doing the best that they can but that they want to help their children as they navigate this often rocky road. There is a fine line, however, between remaining open and pressuring teens to talk about something they prefer to keep private. Parents will need to find this careful balance for themselves.

Remain Honest

Sexuality is a topic about which most people have strong emotions and opinions. It is an intensely personal topic, but parents who remain honest about their own views are ultimately more helpful than those who remain shadowy. Even if a parent's views clash with their teen's, by remaining honest at all times both parties can at least know that they are affording the other the respect of revealing their true thoughts and feelings.

Discussing sex and sexuality with teens may not be the highlight of a parent's life but it is something that every parent should consider. The teenage years can be a confusing time, and despite the fact that modern society often seems saturated with sex our teens still need someone to guide them through this chaotic world.

SEX

If there's one conversation that both parents and teen approach with trepidation it's a talk about sex. However, don't let your dislike for the discussion keep you from imparting information that your teen needs to keep him or herself healthy and safe.

Discuss, Don't Lecture

Teens hate lectures, and they get enough of them in their lives that they know exactly when to tune out if they think a rant or rave is coming. Avoid this inattention by making sure that when you broach the subject of sex you keep it a conversation in which both parties participate. Have a few generic questions ready ("Are kids at your school having sex?" "What do you think of teen pregnancy?") to draw your teen into a discussion and don't interrupt them as they give their answers. Even if what they say surprises you, strive to stay neutral and explore all of their answers without any preconceived notions about what your teen is telling you.

Impart Information

Don't allow your discussion to turn into an interrogation, so make sure that you have information ready to give to your teen regarding safer sex. If your teen thinks that (s)he will have to answer personal questions (s)he may not be comfortable answering then (s)he may not be as receptive to the conversation. Strive to give information that will empower your teen and allow him or her to make informed decisions in the future. Don't delve into personal details about your own sexual experiences, and don't become emotional if your teen does tell you something or voice an opinion that you don't like. Instead, attempt to counter any questionable statements with the facts about sexual health so that you can both leave the conversation confident that you both understand sexual health and safety.

Focus On One Topic

It might seem like having a single conversation in which you touch on all aspects of sex is the best idea – after all, that way you don't need to work up your nerve to have a second, third or fourth discussion. However, the second, third or fourth discussions are exactly what keeps parents and teens on the same page regarding this sensitive topic. Clearing the way for future conversations also keeps the lines of communication open for teens to approach their parents if they have questions or concerns that weren't covered in previous talks. To this end, focus on one topic at a time during each conversation and repeatedly tell your teen that you are always available for future chats. Then, make good on your promises and periodically broach new subjects when you feel the time is right.

Keep a Sense of Humour

It's almost 100% certain that your teen will display some negative emotions during a conversation about sex. Whether it's exasperated sighs, smirks and laughter or eye-rolling and fake shudders, at some point your teen might descend into theatrics that could send the whole conversation off track if you let them. Instead, take it all with a grain of salt. Keep your sense of humour and not only will you be more likely to stay on topic but you might just find that the horrific conversation you were expecting never truly comes to pass

Chapter 12

Tattoos and piercing

Teens of every generation have their fads. Most teenage fads are harmless and eventually fade away without permanent damage. Unfortunately, some of today's most popular fads — particularly tattoos and body piercing — can be permanent and can affect your teen's health. Here are some ideas on how to discuss these fads with your teen:

Don't wait until your child reaches the teen years to talk about tattoos and piercing. Many younger children look up to teens as role models.

Explain the possible dangers of tattoos and piercings, such as infection or allergic reactions. The risk of infection increases if a tattoo or piercing is done under non-sterile conditions.

Ask your teen to imagine how multiple piercings or tattoos might affect his or her future career or relationships.

Explain that a tattoo may not turn out the way you want, and you can't take it back if you don't like it. Further, tattoo removal is very expensive and can be quite painful. In some cases, tattoo removal may cause permanent discoloration of the skin.

Chapter 13

Smoking

We all know smoking is bad in every possible way and that it's certainly not cool to smoke. But each generation has it learn its lessons anew. Your teen might think that smoking looks like the best thing on the planet because some heroes and friends do it.

How do you convince your teen that it's a bad idea? Even more, how do you persuade them of that if you smoke yourself?

Health

By now there should be no doubt about the health dangers of smoking, with increased risk of heart disease, lung cancer, shortness of breath and so on - it's a no-brainer, and billboard advertising helps push the message home.

Ideally, you should have started talking to your kids about smoking when they were young, and reinforcing the message regularly with examples from family and friends. If a relative smoked and died from lung cancer, use that, for instance. It might seem gruesome, but it can be very effective.

If your teen plays sports, remind them that they wouldn't have the lung power to play the same way if they smoked. That can be a powerful tool - remind then that football players, and all athletes, don't smoke.

Point out that smoking is addictive, some say more so than heroin. Ask them if they really want to be a slave to a drug, or whether they'd rather be in control of their own bodies.

Money

Smoking is expensive and becomes more so every year as the tax goes up in each budget. Sit down with your teen and do the maths. Most cigarettes are over £5 for 20. Do they really want to be spending all their pocket money to feed an addiction that will make their clothes stink, their breath smell and which will discolour their teeth? Ask them if they can afford it - the simple, plain truth is that they can't. Don't be gentle about it. Point out just how much it would cost in a year if they smoked 10 cigarettes a day - it's probably far more than they thought.

The Cool Factor

Many teens start smoking because their friends do it or because they think it looks cool. Ask them if they think it's cool to be an addict, because, as smokers, that's what they'd be. If their friends smoke, that doesn't mean they have to. It shows more individualism to say no when offered a cigarette than it does to take it and smoke it. Maybe, you might suggest, it's cooler not to smoke and be the leader - let the others give up and follow your teen instead.

If They Already Smoke

If your teen is already a smoker, don't panic and think all is lost. There are plenty of ways to help them quit, although they'll need the desire to take that step before it can really work. Talk to your GP, who can refer your teen to free NHS quit smoking groups or suggest other strategies. They won't have been smoking long, so the damage won't be too severe, and it shouldn't be too hard to break the addiction.

What If You Smoke

Of course, if you're a smoker and you're urging your teen not to smoke, you can seem like a hypocrite, and that might be pointed out to you. Be willing to admit you were foolish taking it up in the first place, calculate how much you've spent over the years (the amount will probably shock you), and make a pact with your teen - if they don't start, you'll stop.

You know it makes sense for so many reasons, and with the right support, especially encouragement from your teen, you can do it. You'll feel much better when you do stop!

The teenage years are a minefield, not only for the teens themselves, but also for parents - in fact, maybe even more for them. That's because parents know a lot of what to expect, and just how much is involved in being a teenager.

Health is a vital issue. The vast majority of teens have no problems beyond the usual, staying perfectly healthy apart from common bugs. But others can suffer from a variety of things, ranging from meningitis – which isn't just a childhood disease – to anorexia. In many cases there's nothing you can do to prepare your teen for what might happen. All you can do is be there to help them through the illness.

Identifying Teen Health Issues

The big question is what exactly *is* a teen health issue, and the answer is that there isn't one. They overlap childhood and the adult years, so meningitis and juvenile epilepsy can and do occur. But there are also adult issues, such as sexual transmitted infections, body issues (meaning anorexia and bulimia), and a host of other things; they're on the cusp and liable to be hit from both sides.

What Can You Do?

In the event of a serious medical issue, you need to call your doctor or take your teen to an A&E immediately. Don't wait and wonder whether they're really ill, simply go ahead and do it. It's better to be wrong and find they're really not so ill than to procrastinate. In the case of something like meningitis, time is of the essence.

In a number of cases your role will be making sure they get to the GP or to hospital appointments and that they take their medication when prescribed. You might need to nag, but it's important, especially in the case of something like juvenile epilepsy, where medication can help prevent attacks.

You also need to be part of the team educating your teen in the ways to cope with their illness, where it's something requiring ongoing treatment. As the one who's with them most, you're effectively the team leader. If they feel down about the illness, you have to encourage them and be their guide through it all, which isn't easy, and can be a thankless task at times. Sometimes it also involves educating their friends as to what they should do in the event of a seizure, as with epilepsy.

More often it's a case of being there. That might mean visiting them every day in hospital if they're a patient, pampering them a little at home as they recuperate, or just being available to talk or offer company when they need it.

Other Issues

If the problem is something like anorexia or an eating disease, which some girls do suffer from, your role becomes a little different. If your teen isn't hospitalised for treatment, you become part counsellor, part nurse, and, to an extent, part jailer. You have to watch your teen carefully during treatment, encourage and still be firm – it's a difficult balancing act to maintain.

You can certainly try to prevent your teen ever suffering from a sexually transmitted infection by educating them about the dangers of unprotected sex – which, of course, are far greater than pregnancy. Make sure they always carry condoms, just in case, and although you can never be certain they'll use them, encourage them to do so.

Chapter 14

ACNE

Teens and acne…unfortunately, the two just seem to go together. Almost all teens are going to suffer from acne at some point, be it to a greater or lesser degree. There's nothing anyone can do to stop it occurring, it's simply a part of the growing process. Although no one is certain as to the cause of acne, much of it is due to the oil in the skin during adolescence. Stress can also be a factor, so your teen's acne could be worse at exam time.

Teens will get acne and worry about it, as generations of them have done in the past – you almost certainly did yourself. These days, of course, there are plenty of different treatments to help with acne – you only have to open a magazine aimed at teens, regardless of their sex, to see that – but while they can be very effective, there's always more to it than that. Parents can help teens with acne in both practical and emotional ways. It's a difficult enough time for teens anyway, and they need all the support they can get.

Practical Help

The main thing teens want is to be rid of those spots and for them to stay away. You can actually help them long before the problem begins by emphasising how important it is to clean the face properly – which might be a real task with boys. But the cleaner they keep their skin, the less the chance of having a serious acne problem, and the faster spots will clear up. Show them the right way to do it, and be willing to buy them good cleansers. Again, you might have a problem with boys using them, at least until the first outbreak of acne, after which they'll probably become converts.

Keep your eyes open for blackheads on your teen's nose and forehead. These are the first signs of acne, and when you see them, you need to help them take action. The earlier you catch them with a benzoyl peroxide cleanser, the better.

Buy your teen a good over-the-counter benzoyl peroxide cream. In most mild cases of acne, this should clear the face up in just a few days. However, keep an eye on how much they're using it. If they seem to show some side effects, such as a reddening of the skin, suggest they cut back on the treatment somewhat.

Educate your teen about acne, and the fact that popping pimples is a bad idea, however tempting it seems. Point out that they'll actually make the problem worse, making the spots stand out and aggravating, not eliminating, them, although younger teens probably won't listen at first.

Some teens will suffer more than others, and not respond to basic treatment. If yours is one of those, you need to make an appointment with your GP for him or her, and the doctor might, in serious cases, end up referring the teen to a dermatologist who will be able to help. That will be especially traumatic for a teen, so you'll need to be available with encouragement and be willing to talk and support them.

Emotional Support

Teens are very sensitive about their appearance. They see the slightest blemish as a mark that could ruin their lives. Don't belittle that, but don't play into it, either. When they want to talk, be willing to listen, but don't make more of what just be a few spots than they really are.

Without nagging, encourage them to develop a regular daily routine for keeping their skin clean. Make sure they have everything necessary, but leave them the responsibility or remembering and doing it all.

In a very few cases, your teen might have lingering acne scars. There are treatments available to minimise the look of these – consult your GP to find out more.

Chapter 15

Depression and suicide

It is common for teens to occasionally feel unhappy. However, when the unhappiness lasts for more than two weeks and the teen experiences other symptoms (see below), then he or she may be suffering from depression.
There are many reasons why teenagers become unhappy. High-stress environments can lead to depression. Teens can develop feelings of worthlessness and inadequacy over school performance, social interaction, sexual orientation or family life. If friends, family or things that the teen usually enjoys don't help to improve his or her sadness or sense of isolation, there's a good chance that he or she is depressed. Often, depressed teens will display a striking change in their thinking and behaviour, lose their motivation or become withdrawn.
The following are the major signs of depression in adolescents:
Sadness, anxiety or a feeling of hopelessness
Loss of interest in food or compulsive overeating that results in rapid weight loss or gain
Staying awake at night and sleeping during the day n
Withdrawal from friends
Rebellious behaviour, a sudden drop in grades or skipping school
Complaints of pain including headaches, stomach-aches, low back pain or fatigue

Use of alcohol or drugs and promiscuous sexual activity
(These are common ways teens cope with depression.)
A preoccupation with death and dying (This often is a cry for
help and usually indicates a serious case of depression.)
Depression is a serious problem, but it also is treatable. If you
suspect your teen is depressed, tell your child's health care
professional and seek help right away.

Coping with different emotions is part of everyone's life, and
we all feel happy and sad at different times. Sometimes
feeling sad is a natural and appropriate response to what is
happening in our lives. Mostly, we find the passage of time,
life changes and the support of those around us help these
feelings go away.

Depression occurs when sad feelings do not go away, and
when they overwhelm a person and stop them from doing the
things they normally do. It used to be thought that children
and young people couldn't get depressed, but in fact they can,
they may just show it in a different way to adults.

Some of the things that can cause children and young people
to become depressed include:

Parents arguing
Divorce or separation of their parents
The death of someone close to them
Feeling rejected or left out within the family
Problems with school work or exam pressure
Changing school or moving home
Friendship problems
Physical illness in themselves or a carer
Poverty or homelessness.

Suicide is a serious problem within the teen population.
Adolescent suicide is the second leading cause of death
among youth and young adults in the United States. It is
estimated that 500,000 teens attempt suicide, every year with
5,000 succeeding.

Warning signs of suicide include:
Threatening to kill oneself
Preparing for death, giving away favourite possessions, writing goodbye letters or making a will
Expressing a hopelessness for the future
Giving up on oneself, talking as if no one else cares
If your teenager displays any of these behaviours, you should seek help from a mental health professional immediately

Trust is both and emotional and logical act. Emotionally, it is where you expose your vulnerabilities to people, but believing they will not take advantage of your openness. Logically, it is where you have assessed the probabilities of gain and loss, calculating expected utility based on hard performance data, and concluded that the person in question will behave in a predictable manner. In practice, trust is a bit of both. I trust you because I have experienced your trustworthiness and because I have faith in human nature.

We feel trust. Emotions associated with trust include companionship, friendship, love, agreement, relaxation, comfort.

There are a number of different ways we can define trust. Here are the dimensions of trust and consequent definitions.

Definition 1: Trust means being able to predict what other people will do and what situations will occur. If we can surround ourselves with people we trust, then we can create a safe present and an even better future.

It is a normal part of the human condition to be constantly forecasting ahead. We build internal models of the world based both on our experiences and what others tell us, and then use these to guess what will happen next. This allows us to spot and prepare for threats and also make plans to achieve our longer-term goals.

The greatest unpredictability is at 50%; a reliable enemy can be preferable to an unpredictable friend, as at least we know where we are with them.

Guilt

Guilt is a natural emotion that comes as a result of the person doing something that is against his or her values.

It is like a built-in self-correction system that notifies you the second you get out of harmony with what you consider right or wrong.

Many people wrongly interpret guilt thinking that guilt is a notification of a sin.

Because of this reason some people stay in this emotion until they get depressed and feel unworthy. Guilt, however, was never intended to be interpreted this way. Guilt should not be dwelled in, its only purpose is to notify you of your deviation from your values.

Anger

Anger is a natural emotion that every human and many non-human animals experience. Mild forms of human anger may include displeasure, irritation or dislike. When we react to frustration, criticism or a threat, we may become angry - and usually this is a healthy response. Anger may be a secondary response to feeling sad, lonely or frightened. When anger becomes a full-blown rage our judgment and thinking can become impaired and we are more likely to do and say unreasonable and irrational things.

Anger is not just a mental state of mind. It triggers an increase in heart rate, blood pressure and levels of adrenaline and noradrenaline. Anger has survival benefits, and forms part of our *fight or flight* brain response to a perceived threat or harm. When a human or animal decides to take action to stop or confront a threat, anger usually becomes the predominant feeling and takes over our behavior, cognition and physiology.

In many cases humans and non-human animals express anger by making loud sounds, baring teeth, staring and specific posturing as a warning to perceived aggressors to stop their threatening behaviours'. It is unusual for a physical attack to occur without these signs of anger appearing first. If a stranger approaches some newborn puppy-dogs the mother will most likely growl, bare her teeth and adopt a defensive or ready-to-attack posture, rather than silently attack without any warning. If you trespass into the private land of a farmer in a remote area, his approach may be similar; his voice may be hostile, as may his body language, and posture. Instinctively, anger may surge in humans and non-human animals to protect territory, offspring and family members, secure mating privileges, prevent loss of possessions or food, and many other perceived threats.

Experts say anger is a primary, natural emotion with functional survival value, which we all experience from time to time. The raised heart rate, blood pressure, and release of hormones prepare us physically for remedial action - which is either to fight or run away at top speed (fight or flight).

Being a parent and bringing up children is not an easy task, in fact in many ways it is the hardest job you may ever have because there is such a wealth of conflicting advice and information available.

Family Advice

You may well find that friends and family all want to share with you the benefit of their advice, gleaned from many years of experience of bringing up children, but ultimately the way you raise your children and help your family to grow and develop is up to you, your own standards, boundaries, ideas and plans for the future of you and your children.

It is often difficult to know exactly what parenting methods and styles to adopt and you may find that you are questioning yourself on a regular basis about certain aspects of your children's development! This is never helped by spending too much time with competitive friends who may appear to be well meaning with their tips and advice, but who can also make life even more stressful!

Chapter 16

Parenting Has Changed

There is no doubt that the way we bring up our children is definitely changing, and while your parents and grandparents may have had one style of parenting, this may not fit in well with the expectations you now have as a parent yourself.
One of the best known specialists in parenting styles is Diana Baumrind and she had four distinct categories for describing the ways that people parent their children. So are you a permissive, authoritarian or assertive-democratic parent?
Permissive Parenting
If you basically allow your child to have a lot of freedom, consult them about everything that is happening in your household and make very few demands on them when it comes to helping with chores, then you are probably a permissive parent. This style of parenting became popular after the war when children were first encouraged to think for themselves, and the old 'children should be seen and not heard' approach started to change.
Although children raised in this style can be creative and original, they often have trouble fitting in because they lack boundaries and in basic terms have been allowed to get away with bad behaviour. They often struggle to fit in at school because they have little or no idea about the real difference between right and wrong, and often have poor social skills because other children find their behaviour difficult to cope with.
Authoritarian Parenting
Authoritarian parents on the other hand, adopt a style that involves having too much control over their children. Their focus is often on ensuring that they display positive behaviour at all times, and are actively involved with helping around the house. Children are kept firmly in their place, and there really

is no room for arguing. In this case, the parents' word is law! This extreme approach to parenting is very traditional and now considered to be largely outdated and unnecessary.

Assertive-Democratic Parenting
Assertive-democratic parents however, spend their time working hard to make sure some basic boundaries are established for their children and they actively encourage them to take responsibility for what they have done, while at the same time giving them lots of opportunities to make their own independent choices.
Bad behaviour is usually dealt with by using time out, and saying sorry and making up are all part of the process.
Assertive-democratic parenting is the best for today's children as they learn to accept responsibility, make wiser choices and cope with change really well. This is because they have basic and simple boundaries in place in their lives.
Baumrind also identified neglectful parenting in her research - in other words parents who either do not wish to interact with their children, or who simply, for whatever reason, cannot interact - instead simply managing to fulfil basic responsibilities and duties of care, but with little concern for the development of their child.
Loving, Secure Parenting
Although parenting styles may have changed over the years, the basic job of parents remains the same, and we have a responsibility to ensure our children have loving, secure homes in which to grow and develop into well balanced, adjusted, reasonable, sociable and happy young people who have much to contribute to society.

Parenting is not something that has hard and fast rules, and over the course of your child's life you may well find that the way you raise your family changes and evolves.
Parenting styles

However without even realising it you will adopt a parenting style that has its origins deeply rooted in research work carried out by the child behaviour and psychology expert Diana Baumrind. Baumrind's work and the origins of parenting styles have shaped the way that millions of people have raised their children over the last century and continue to do so today.

The research behind the development of Diana Baumrind's parenting styles was based on two aspects of parenting that she considered to be extremely important, and this is how parenting styles were first analysed and labelled.

Parental Responsiveness

The first aspect of parenting was known as Parental Responsiveness, and refers to how much the parent is prepared to respond to the child's needs. The second was called Parental Demandingness. This term is used to examine the level to which the parent expects and anticipates a more grown up, sensible and ultimately responsible level and standard of behaviour from their child.

Recognised Strategies

In simple terms, a Parenting Style is a way that experts use to describe certain standard and recognised strategies or concepts that all parents use in raising their children. In other words, a parenting style is the way that you choose to bring up your children, and it may well differ from the styles your parents used and those used by your friends, however in modern society many parents adopt elements of the same style and just adjust them to suit the behaviour of their individual children.

Authoritative

Many parents adopt the authoritative parenting approach and the origins of this style are based on instilling important values into a child such as self discipline, emotional self control, a wide and secure social circle and even achieving more positive results at school. This approach can benefit children as it also lead to them having a good level of self esteem and self confidence, whilst also being aware of the importance of boundaries and reacting to those boundaries in a positive rather than rebellious way.

Huge Benefit

Research that has been carried out into the different styles of parenting has demonstrated clearly that authoritative parenting has a huge benefit to children; however, when discipline is taken to the extreme, this can have a negative effect on children and in turn encourage them to adopt a harsher regime than is necessary with their own children.

Useful Tools

The origins of Baumrind's specific parenting styles are useful tools for all parents to examine the way they are raising their children, and by examining each method and the effect that a parents' behaviour directly has on their children, we are able to establish our own individual parenting styles that suit the individual needs of our children.

Traditional Values

The way that we raise our children has changed a lot over the last 50 years or so, but traditional values continue to remain important both socially and behaviourally and parents across the world draw on Baumrind's research and analysis every day as they try to instil core values into their children that will help their development and encourage positive behaviour and secure, confident children.

There really isn't a right or wrong way to bring up children, and although there are thousands of books, websites, magazines and even DVDs on the subject of parenting, you will find that they all make one thing crystal clear-every child is different and has different needs, behaviour patterns and therefore requires a different approach.

With such a wealth of information available, and with parenting becoming increasingly competitive, it is understandable why so many of us struggle on a daily basis with knowing what to do for the best!

Establish Your Style

A good way to start to look at your parenting skills is to establish your parenting style because this will give you a good indication of what is working and what clearly is not, and from then on you can make some adjustments and changes that could actually make a big difference to the way your child responds to you.

Parenting styles fall into the following categories:

• **Authoritarian• Authoritative• Permissive• Neglectful or uninvolved**

Questions...

Here are a few questions that you could ask yourself to try and establish the kind of parent you are, and whether or not your parenting style is working for your children:

1. If your child hits another child in the playground, how do you react?

a. Get really angry and tell the other child to hit your child back?

b. Ignore both of the children and Just let them get on with it?

c. Make it clear to your child that hitting is not acceptable behaviour, make sure they apologise and if it happens again remove a privilege?

2. Your child and some friends have made a huge mess in his bedroom but now want to go outside and play. Do you:

a. Shout at them and make them clear it up?

b. Just let them go and play and deal with the mess yourself?

c. Invent a game that involves clearing up and get involved yourself?

3. One of your children is trying hard to get out of going to bed by claiming to be hungry. Do you:

a. Get cross and make her got to bed, even if she is hungry?

b. Let her have whatever she wants to eat?

c. Choose a healthy snack for her to have but make it clear that she should have eaten more at supper time?

4. If your children have temper tantrums, do you:

a. Get cross and send them to their bedrooms?

b. Give in and let them do whatever they like because it's easier that way?

c. Stand your ground but try and make them understand that there are better ways to express how they are feeling?

5. If one of your children wakes you in the night because they are having a bad dream, do you:

a. Get angry because they have woken you up?

b. Let them sleep wherever they like?

c. Make sure they are OK and stay with them until they fall asleep?

6. The main reason for parenting and discipline is to:

a. Make sure that your children know they must listen to you ALWAYS?

b. Make sure that everyone is happy and doing what they want?

c. Teach your children the importance of rules and boundaries, and encourage them to make good choices independently?

Mostly A's - Authoritarian
An authoritarian parent tries to control a child's behaviour and insists that they have complete respect for authority; they are not very flexible in their approach to parenting and will sometimes resort to smacking or hitting a child if they do not behave. They often display anger and shout at their children.
Mostly B's- Permissive

A permissive parent is extremely laid back and relaxed about their child's behaviour and does not insist on boundaries or even a particular standard of behaviour, preferring to keep everyone happy rather than using any form of discipline or authority.

Mostly C's- Authoritative

An authoritative parent believes that both the child and the parent's needs are important and need to be met and that they both have certain rights. The parent is in control and doesn't need to use physical force to keep the child well behaved, because they are more likely to control the child by setting rules and explaining why they are

Demandingness and Responsiveness

Parenting essentially falls into two categories and these are known as Demandingness and Responsiveness. These elements describe the kind of reaction that parents can be expected to have based on the behaviour of their children. These two labels can then be used to categories the kind of parenting style of individuals, and those parenting styles are

Authoritarian: Strict, old fashioned and not at all flexible

Permissive (also known as the indulgent parenting style): Too laid back in most cases and children often suffer from a lack of boundaries

Authoritative: Assertive and responsive parents, the most well balanced approach to parenting in general

Neglectful or dismissive: Exert little care or consideration for their children

The parenting styles are also influenced by certain psychological issues by making children feeling guilty, isolated, withdrawal of loving behaviour or by children being made to feel ashamed and humiliated by their behaviour.

Psychology

A major difference between authoritarian and authoritative parenting concerns psychology. Although authoritarian and authoritative parents both put high demands on their children and expect good behaviour. Authoritarian parents, also expect their children to accept their decisions without questioning them. However, authoritative parents are more open to a bit of give and take with their children.

Research has shown that parenting styles do have a direct effect and influence on the behaviour, general well being and development of children in the following contexts:

Behaviourally

Socially

Academic achievements

Career/work progression

Self esteem/confidence

Children who are raised by authoritative parenting measures tend to have high self esteem, where as children whose parents are neglectful tend not to thrive or develop at the same rate. Those from authoritarian families perform reasonably well at school but often have lower social skills, lower self esteem and often high levels of depression. Those who are from permissive or indulgent homes can suffer because they can't cope with the school environment as well, but often have better self esteem and cope well in some social situations where boundaries are not required.

The majority of parents adopt a number of parenting styles and methods, preferring to look at their child as an individual rather than following a definite style of bringing up their children that they may have read about.

The most old fashioned and outdated of all of Diana Baumrind's parenting styles has to be the authoritarian approach to bringing up children. Parents who adopt this style of parenting have often been raised in the same way by their parents and have extremely high standards of behaviour and respect.

Authoritarian Parenting

Authoritarian parents focus on shaping, controlling and evaluating the behaviour of their children by using a set code of conduct that is based on the child having total respect for authority.

Parents place a high value on obedience as a good thing, and will use forceful measures to ensure that their child's behaviour is maintained at all times. This type of parents shows little flexibility, and children are very much kept in their place.

Children are given very strict boundaries and guidelines for behaviour and how they should live their lives, and are not really considered in decision making processes as they are not given choices or encouraged to make their own decisions.

Respect for Authority

Authoritarian parenting involves keeping children in their place, having restricted autonomy, and household chores, jobs and duties figure highly on their agenda. Children who are parented using this style are given jobs to do around the house, as parents believe that having this level of responsibility will encourage the child to have respect for adults and therefore a certain standard of behaviour will be maintained at all times.

Parents who use this style of parenting do not encourage any level of discussion or give and take, basically their word is law and their children have no choice but to do as they are told. Children are told that they must do as they are told and there is no flexibility or discussion allowed about any situations that may arise within the family unit.

Control And Responsibility

Authoritarian parenting involves being in control and exerting that control on their children. Parents who set these strict rules do it to keep order and do this without any warm emotion or affection. They try hard to set standards of behaviour and are harshly critical of their children if they fail to meet those standards. They actively tell their children what to do and how to behave, and their children have to accept it.

Authoritarian parents tend to be unable to explain their children why they want them to do things. Authoritarian parents don't explain why they want their children to do things. If their children question a rule the parent would probably say, "Because I said so, do as I say." Authoritarian parents tend to focus on bad behaviour, rather than good behaviour, and children are often harshly punished and told off, for not following their strict rules.

Children who are subjected to authoritarian parenting rarely learn to think for themselves and struggle to understand why their parents behave the way they do. Authoritarian parenting is out dated and not suited to modern life and society, it is not considered to be an appropriate parenting style for today's family.

Permissive parenting is at the other end of the spectrum from the authoritarian parenting style, and basically allows children to grow up in an environment of extreme freedom and flexibility.

Permissive Parenting

While authoritarian parents rule their children with a rod of iron, permissive parenting styles allow children to have a huge amount of input into how the family home and environment develops, and they are seldom called upon to help or get involved with any chores or domestic responsibilities, leaving any jobs or duties firmly in the hands of the parents.

This is the parents' choice and they feel comfortable and secure in the knowledge that they are providing a firm foundation on which their children can grow and develop. They do not feel that being involved in such mundane activities, or having any level of responsibility is important to the way that children are raised.

No Boundaries Is Not Necessarily Good...

A childhood without any boundaries or responsibility can be as damaging as one with too many, and permissive parenting can result in children who struggle with environments where boundaries have to exist, such as school and the workplace. Children who have been raised in a permissive parenting style are often creative and successful academically, and can be sociable but can also find that problems will exit within their social circles as they do not always understand or respond well to mainstream behaviour-something that everyone else is used to. Permissive parenting allows children to have their own way over almost anything and it is for this reason that children may struggle at school.

A Household with Few Rules

Permissive parents want to and tend to give up most control of the home and family life to their children. Parents make very few rules, and even when they do decide to make a rule, the rules that they make are usually not enforced all the time or properly. Parents who adopt this style of parenting do not like or respond well to routines. They want their children to feel as if they can be free to do or say as they wish and have as much freedom as they need to live their lives the way they want to.

Behaviour Is Accepted

Permissive parents rarely have high expectations or proper boundaries and guidelines for the way they want their children to behave, whether at home, in social circumstances or at school, and they are always inclined to accept their children and their behaviour- whether it is good or bad. Basically-there are very few rules with permissive parenting.

Choices Are Given

Permissive parents give children as many choices as they possibly can, even when they know in their heart that their child is not even capable of making choices-be they good or bad. Behaviour patterns and the way that children react to any given circumstances are nearly always accepted, and permissive parents are unlikely to ever make a comment about whether they consider their child's behaviour to be an action that will have desirable or undesirable outcomes.

Rather than discipline their child, permissive parents tend to keep a safe distance from any kind of confrontation, situation requiring a firm hand or other situations that require intervention. The reason for this is twofold-firstly they choose not to believe that children require a high level of supervision or help with their behaviour or decision making, and secondly because they often have an inability to be able to interject.

Progressive Education

Permissive parents would welcome the idea of progressive education, where children attend schools that they have control of. They believe that children should be free to learn, grow and develop at their own pace without the restrictions and boundaries that our modern day culture and society has placed on them.

Assertive Democratic Parenting Style is also often known and referred to by experts as the Authoritative parenting style. Assertive Democratic parenting produces children who are generally well balanced and able to cope with situations well. It is a parenting style that is adopted by many parents as it is a reasonable way for parents to manage expectations and encourage and reward good, positive behaviour.

Encourage Responsibility

Children are actively encouraged from a reasonably early age to be responsible for themselves and to be able to think clearly about their behaviour and the effect it can have on other people and situations.

Parents who adopt this style of parenting achieve their aims and objectives by making sure their children have very clear and simple expectations for their children. They ensure that they always explain things to their children, and make it clear to them that they expect a certain level and standard of behaviour, and why those standards are so important.

Consistent Advice

Assertive Democratic or Authoritative parents always keep a close eye on their children's behaviour and try to make sure that their advice to their children is consistent. They make big efforts to try and observe their children when they are being good so that this positive behaviour can be rewarded. By regularly reinforcing their children's good behaviour and making a big deal about rewarding them, Assertive Democratic parents try not to focus on negative behaviour.

Explanations and behaviour

When their children do not behave themselves, Assertive Democratic parents explain to them why they are not happy with their behaviour and try to help them to understand the repercussions that their actions may have on others, particularly if their behaviour may injure another child. These way children learn from an early age that they have to demonstrate a certain level of responsibility for their actions.

Help Around the House

Children who have Assertive Democratic parents will be encouraged to get involved with helping around the house with domestic chores. Families like this will often have a family rota or schedule with everyone having their own list of jobs to do during the week. Decisions about the kind of job that each child will be given, will depend on their age and ability-there is a strong focus on rewarding a child for good or positive behaviour and therefore it is important that they will be able to achieve the task they are asked to perform.

Choices Are Important

Assertive Democratic parents like to offer their children choices and again these are dependent on the age and ability of each child. A preschool child might be given the option of what to wear, in other words "a red shirt or a blue shirt?" whereas older children might be given the choice of what to eat, or what to play.

As children progress through the education system, their choices of GCSEs and A levels will become hot topics of conversation, and by this stage these children will have developed into well-balanced and confident young people who have excellent communication and decision making capabilities.

Assertive Democratic parents do not allow the large amount of freedom that permissive parents deem to be acceptable, and neither do they adopt the rather old-fashioned and outdated approach of the authoritarian parent. Instead, they prefer to look at each child as an individual and allow them the room and opportunities to grow and develop. There is a firm focus on cultivating independence from an early age, ensuring children remain aware of the outcomes of their actions and behaviour, and being able to cope well and thrive in any social setting.

What Teenage Rebellion Means

Teenage rebellion is a rite of passage, a movement from childhood to the adulthood, a way of establishing an individual identity both within the family and in society. It can take many forms, from haircuts and a general look to an attitude that is often confrontational, especially at home. After having once accepted the boundaries you've set as a parent, the growing child now needs to establish new ones, and part of that will be to see how far you can be pushed. A word of warning - after spending their whole lives with you, they instinctively know which buttons to push and what can rile you.

How to React

The best advice is to never let yourself react hastily, although that's not always possible. At some point your teen will wind you up beyond your patience and you'll explode. Its' going to happen. But as far as possible, keep control, however frustrating the teen can be.

Talk things through, and don't criticise the new odd hairstyle or clothes. Do they actually harm anyone? You might not like them, but are they really a problem in the great scheme of things? You'll have your battles during the teenage years, but pick them wisely, don't go after every little thing.

Of course, there are limits. When behaviour becomes dangerous - drinking heavily or drug taking - then you have to speak out forcefully, for the sake of the teen and your family. Otherwise, though, just be as patient, and as forgiving, as you can.

Your teen might still be your baby, but don't treat them that way. Once they're teenagers it's no longer cute, it's condescending. Treat them as adults, which is how they see themselves. It doesn't mean you have to be their best friend (indeed, that's not advisable, you need that distance), but don't talk down to them. Discuss issues sensibly and sanely, treat their opinions with respect.

What to Expect

There's no hard and fast time when the rebellion sets in, or even what form it can take. Rather than being taken by surprise when it arrives, though, expect it to come and keep your eyes open. That will certainly help your patience when it all bursts forth.

Remember, your teens are trying to find their place in this world, and pushing against things and people is a way to create space and be noticed, to establish who they are. In other words, they're even more confused by all this than you are.

For what it's worth, this is just a stage or phase and it will pass, although it can seem endless when they're going through it.

Behaviour can be a problem. They'll be more argumentative and very defensive or their positions and who they are. Accept that, and where possible try to avoid confrontation. In the end it serves no purpose other than to push the two of you further apart.

Teens can be moody, angry and rebellious, among many other things, and parents become used to dealing with lightning-fast changes in temperament. In fact, parents can become desensitised to what might really be going on because of all this. What's written off as just teenage behaviour can be making something deeper, darker and more dangerous – serious depression, for instance, or heavy alcohol use or drug taking.

But how does a parent distinguish between teenage behaviour and problem behaviour?

The First Warning Signs

First of all, there can be many warning signs, and it's impossible to offer a complete list, it will vary from person to person. But these general indicators can at least raise red flags, meaning a parent should talk to their teen and to others – teachers or doctors – who might be able to help or give more indication as to what to look for.

They might seem erratic to you, but your teen will have routines and habits. If these suddenly change in any drastic manner, which could well be a warning that something is going on. The same applies to sleep. Teens like to sleep, and staying in bed until midday on the weekends isn't uncommon. But if that begins when they've generally been early risers, and they don't seem to be keeping especially late hours, keep your eyes open for something wrong.

If their schoolwork goes downhill, and especially if they begin skipping school, there's probably something going on in their lives you need to address. Apart from the legal obligations of making sure they attend school, it forms a central routine in their lives and provides them with the education they need for the future.

Teens can be very private about their activities, but if the secrecy seems excessive, if they lie to you often about what they've been doing, or if they take up with new friends whom you think far from suitable (and not just because of their appearance), it should be a cause for worry. It could be an indicator of bad things happening.

Real Danger Signs

Even excellent parents can miss warning signs if the teens are tricky enough. However, if things escalate, you can still spot it early enough to head off real disaster.

If you find drugs or things associated with drugs (if you don't know what those might be, it's worthwhile educating yourself on the subject) around your teen, you need to take immediate action before it goes too far.

Similarly, if they don't shower for a week, for instance, or wear the same clothes for days on end until they stink, then something is definitely wrong. Talk to them and seek help for them.

Behaviour can give great clues. If they suddenly appear reckless, don't care about anything, whether they're destructive or self-destructive, find help for them immediately – that's especially true in cases of self-harm, such as cutting themselves or being truly threatening. If the behaviour has veered far from the person you knew, it might well be because they need help for different issues.

If you find that your teen has weapons, such as a knife or even a gun, don't be afraid to call the police. You might feel you're betraying them, but in the long run you'll be doing them a favour.

The teenage years can be difficult, more so now than when you experienced them, and there are many pressures on teens that didn't exist before. They react to them in different ways. Watching them, and getting them help when they need it, is the act of a loving parent, not an interfering one.

You're going to argue with your teen. Just take that as a given. It might happen often, it might happen rarely, but it will happen. As they test their limits – and test you – you'll butt heads.

Most of the time, the heat passes in a few minutes and life reverts more or less to normal. But sometimes the arguments can escalate into blazing rows and go on and on. In a few instances they can also lead to violence. What do you do then?

Arguments

It's not easy, but try to keep calm during arguments with your teen. However, it's worthwhile, otherwise you can end up saying things that both of you will regret. Accept that your teen will argue, and will make hurtful comments. Most of the time they don't mean them, it's just a reaction.

But when the arguments become more serious and deeper – which can happen out of the blue – you still need to stay calm, and, if possible, calm your teen down, too. Try to defuse the situation. Don't make inflammatory remarks. In fact, be as conciliatory as possible, with empathetic remarks such as "I see what you mean on that" or "I understand how you feel." Encourage them to talk, rather than shout.

It won't always work, especially if they have a lot of anger inside, and some teens are powder kegs of anger and frustration. In those instances, you can try walking away as a method of lessening the tension – say something like "You seem very angry, do you think it would be better if we talked later?" Ultimately, though, you can't ignore the situation. If your teen is that worked up, you need to do something about it.

If real anger is a regular occurrence, you should sit and talk to your teen about counselling. Obviously there's a problem, and an objective professional who's not involved on a day-to-day basis might be able to help discover and solve it. A number of people do have anger management issues, and if you can help resolve them before they become serious, the better your teen will be.

Bear in mind that often your teen doesn't have the emotional and developmental maturity to deal with anger, and letting it out is all they can do. There are techniques that can be taught that can help with cope with the problems.

Violence

If arguments reach the stage of violence, with your teen hitting out, either at people or objects, then it's time to seek help.

It's not normal or even acceptable behaviour, and coping with it can be difficult. The temptation is to try and calm the teen, but at this stage that's often not possible, especially if you're the one being attacked.

The best advice is to get out of there. You have to look out for your own safety. In many cases, the teen isn't attacking you personally, but simply using violence as a way to get rid of anger and frustration – you just happen to be the closest person at the time.

But it's symptomatic of much deeper problems that need to be treated. You should call the police if you believe if you're in danger, but it can often be better to remove yourself and let the anger burn itself out.

Once calmness has returned, talk to your teen about what's happened. They might not even know why they did it. Forgive them, point out that they're posing a danger to themselves, as well as others, and suggest talking to someone about it – then make an appointment as soon as you can.

Work with the counsellor and your teen wherever possible. It's a difficult, trying time for you and your teen, but working on these issues can help create a strong, lifelong bond between you.

Discipline

Just like children, teens need discipline, although they'd probably never admit it or even consciously think it. But, like their younger siblings, they do benefit from structure and routine, and being taken to task when they don't obey the rules. Like everyone else, they have to be reminded that rules, both within the family and in society, are part of the order of life, and that there are punishments for flouting them.

However, you can't punish a teen the way you would a four-year-old. What are the options as a parent, and what should you discipline and what should you ignore?

What to Punish

Teens tend to be a moody, sometimes surly group, and, depending on the teen, often in the mood for an argument about the most minor thing. As a parent you have to learn not to take offence or react to every little incident. It's exhausting and simply not worth it; you'll end up battling your teen all the time.

Pick your battles, the areas where you have to take a stand. Remember, part of your job is to help them take responsibility for their lives and guide them towards adulthood and independence.

Set up guidelines with your teen over what is acceptable behaviour and what is not. The boundaries will differ from person to person. You might not find excessive rudeness acceptable, for instance, where someone else might tolerate it. Decide where to set the boundaries and make sure they're firmly described and defined to your teen.

What Punishments Should You Set?

It can be easy to overreact to an incident or event and set an excessive punishment in the hope the teen will never do it again. That's never a good strategy – all you do is end up creating a climate of secrecy, where things won't come into the open for fear of punishment.

Let the discipline fit the crime. If your teen has a time to be home and is late, without notification or an excellent excuse, then refuse them permission to go out the following night. It's fair, and your teen will understand that – although they'll still complain.

Grounding them for a month simply won't work. If they've done something so bad you feel it deserves that, then you need to look at why they did and address the cause more than inflict such a harsh punishment.

Stay calm, and take the time to think before you set a punishment (but don't draw it out or say "Wait until your father gets home," for instance). Be as rational and objective as you can.

Don't use sarcasm as punishment. It's not a mature way to deal with things.

Removing privileges hits your teen where they live. Refusing lifts for a certain period, not letting them do certain activities they enjoy and refusing them permission to attend a party or see their boyfriend or girlfriend can all be very effective tools.

Be prepared to re-negotiate boundaries and limits as your teen gets older. It allows them to take more responsibility, and shows that you're willing to trust them more.

When your teen rants and raves about a punishment, don't take it personally. As with the moody behaviour, it's not directed at you, it's just an expression of frustration.

You should also be consistent. Don't let something go once then punish it the next time. If it's a rule, you need to apply it every time.

Talk to your teen about what they've done wrong and possibly more importantly, why they've done it. Good communication can stop a lot of problems.

As any parent of a teen will tell you, teens are moody creatures. They can shift from happy to surly to sad in seconds, and for no apparent reason. Unfortunately, as their nearest and dearest, you have to deal with it, which can make for trying times. One minute you can be having a normal conversation and the next you might as well be talking to the wall.

Why does it happen and what can you do about it?

Why Teens Are Moody

Although teens are said to have raging hormones in terms of sex, it actually applies much more to their personalities. Those crazy mood swings are purely a product of hormones, according to studies.

They can't control it, and, just as they're baffled and confused by all the changes going on in their bodies, they're confused by what's going on emotionally, too. They don't know when their moods will change, or why, and there's absolutely nothing they can do about it.

Think about that for a minute. If the wild mood swings seem bad enough for you, on the outside of things, imagine what it must be like to be on the inside, to have a mind that seems determined to go its own way. It can be terrifying.

What Can You Do About It?

The brief answer is – you can't do anything to stop it. It is going to happen, regardless. All you can do is live with it. In a way, some of the moodiness, especially when they seem to be pushing you away, are part of the process by which they become individuals, and that necessitates rejecting their parents a little.

What you can do is make sure that you don't reject them when they're rejecting you. They don't really mean it, so make sure you stay calm and loving. Give them space, it's what they need, but don't push them away.

The time to talk to your teen is, quite obviously, when they're not in a mood. Don't get into a fight with them when they're moody. It will resolve nothing, and you'll both end up feeling frustrated and with more fences to mend.

Be supportive, not judgemental. Talk to them about school, their lives and friends, and really listen to what they have to say. If your teen wants to talk, make time, don't put it off until later. Gentle humour can be a powerful tool, helping them laugh at their mistakes, but be warned, it's easy to tip over the edge into belittling them, so be careful.

Reassure them that you support them and you'll be there for them, no matter what. It can be a time of low self-esteem, and they need that sort of back-up to help them approach the world with more confidence.

They're slowly spreading their wings and learning to fly. They need that and it's part of the process of growing up. But set limits with even the moodiest teen, and punish them if they defy those limits.

When Is It Moody And When Is It Depression?
Sometimes it can be hard to tell when a teen is just moody and when he or she is tumbling into depression. Moods pass like rain, but depression stays around. Watch for warning signs like excessive sleeping, marks slipping at school, inattention to personal hygiene and others. If you sense it might be depression, talk to your teen seriously and then to your GP

It may be that you feel your teen needs counselling, that the problems they have are beyond your ability and that you need the help of a professional in dealing with them.

There's nothing to be ashamed of in that, in fact, quite the opposite. You're making a step in the right direction, and quite possibly doing the best thing for your teen. If you think of counselling as a bad thing, an admission of defeat or mental problems, don't.

Seeking help is a good thing, and there really are problems we can't manage alone. Counsellors are trained, qualified professionals. The odds are that they'll have dealt with situations like yours before, and in the vast majority of cases, they can help.

In fact, more than any other group, teens may benefit from counselling, because during such a transitional stage there are so many issues that bother them, and they may well find it easier to open up to someone who's not a part of their life or social circle, but who can still understand.

Issues Involving Counselling

The main issue causing parents to seek counselling for a teen is behaviour. It may seem past your control, with excessive drinking, drug taking, or doing things that simply aren't acceptable in society.

More and more, obesity is becoming an issue that counsellors are handling.

Don't feel you've failed as a parent because your teen needs counselling. If anything, it's the opposite; by seeking help you're going one step beyond what many parents would do to create a successful life and future for your offspring.

First Steps

Finding a good counsellor is an art, not a science. If you know others parents whose teens have undergone counselling, ask them for recommendations. Ask at school and your GP.

Rather than simply making an appointment, talk to the counsellor first, have a session with them. It gives you a chance to lay out the problem as you see it (your view and your teens will probably be strikingly different), and also gives your more opportunity to judge whether your teen will benefit from this particular counsellor.

Persuading your teen to see a counsellor might not be easy. They may feel it's not necessary, or feel that it'll become a stigma if word gets out. Be gentle about it, ask if they'll just sit and talk to this person. Explain that you're having problems coping, and that this will help you.

How You Can Help

Unless specifically requested by the counsellor or the teen, it's best of you don't sit in on the sessions. After all, the idea is to give your teen space to express doubts and fears on the issues involved.

However, at some point you might be asked to participate, and it can be very helpful, addressing the concerns through a third party. The thing to avoid is confrontation with your teen. Be considered in your words, but listen to what they say. If they've established a good level of trust with the counsellor, you might hear things you haven't heard before, but don't react angrily, no matter how harsh it is. Remember, these are genuine concerns on the part of your teen and need to be addressed seriously in order to help remedy the problem.

Be available to your teen. You don't need to pry into what was discussed when you weren't there, but be willing to talk openly at home, even if it doesn't come easily. It will help them become better adults.

Chapter 17

The Internet

Computers, especially those with an Internet connection, have become a part of modern life. Every day teens use them to do homework, research, keep in touch with friends, listen to music, watch television programmes and movies and generally entertain themselves. But when is enough an enough? How do you know if your teen has a healthy interest in electronics or has become addicted to the computer? Continue reading for some clues to help you determine if your teen's computer use has become addictive.

Time

One of the first things to think about in relation to a teen's computer use is how much time (s) he spends on the computer each day. This will obviously vary per person, but in general if a teen is spending more than an hour or two on the computer then it is likely that (s) he is missing out on other parts of life. Also think about the time of day that a teen is on the computer. If a teen comes home from school and heads to the computer to do homework this is one thing, but if a teen waits until the family has gone to bed to begin his or her computer use then it is quite another.

Purpose

Do you know why your teen is using the computer? If you ask your teen, will they tell you? These are two questions that any parent should be asking in regards to teen computer use. As a general rule of thumb, teens who can immediately and articulately describe why they use the computer usually do have a reason to be on them. However, teenagers who are vague or secretive about their computer use may have no reason to be on the computer other than because they are addicted or fear living their life away from the machine.

Other Activities

In addition to using the computer, can you think of activities that your teen enjoys and engages in regularly? If so, then it is likely that your teen has a fairly balanced life. If not, then it is likely that your teen is sacrificing or otherwise missing out on a well rounded life for the sake of spending time on the computer. Though extra computer use may be acceptable at certain times (for example, during school holidays), in general it should not take up so much time that it precludes a teen from engaging in other activities.

Electronic communication has become a way of life for teens, from sending text messages to instant messaging to sending emails. However, there is a difference between electronic communication that complements face-to-face communication and electronic communication that is used instead of face-to-face communication. Talk to your teen about his or her friends. Are they available in real life or do you have a sneaking suspicion that your teen has only online friends? Do you think your teen is following proper Internet safety methods or do you fear that (s)he may be disclosing sensitive information to these new friends? Does your teen ever meet his or her friends off line? Is this a common occurrence? The more you ponder your teen's friendships the more you may realise about his or her computer use.

In general, teens love technology and a computer has become a fact of life for these youngsters. If you fear that your teen has become addicted to the computer, think about the time (s)he spends on it, the purpose for which (s)he logs on, if (s)he engages in other activities and who (s)he counts as friends. These variables usually give parents a well-rounded picture of a teen's computer use and enough information to decide if their teen seems to be addicted to the computer.

Peer pressure can be a formidable force whether it comes from specific individuals or general pop culture. However, by discussing pop culture with your teen you'll not only be opening the channels of communication between yourselves but can seize on the opportunity to bond over some of the cultural developments as well. As long as you use these discussions to reiterate your family values there's not much more that parents can do. At some point teens need to go out into the world and deal with the pop culture of the moment. You'll just have to be confident that you've taught your teen well and his or her choices will make you proud.

Discussing Pop Culture
"Pop culture" is a term that is used to mean popular culture. That is, the popular items such as books, films, fashions, sports, music, foods and more those are popular at a given time. These items are usually circulating widely around the community or country so they are readily recognisable for those who are up to the minute about trends.
Discussing pop culture with your teen can be tricky simply because it moves so quickly. Just when you think you know the names of a popular musician you'll find out that someone else has come up and taken his or her place.
By the time you have a chance to watch a film on DVD there will be another blockbuster raking in millions at the cinema. Don't let the fear of being outdated stop you from having important discussions, however. Admit to your teen that you may not be up totally au fait with every aspect of pop culture, but that there are certain aspects that are worrying you. This will give you the perfect platform to begin a general discussion, whether it be about drink, drugs, teen pregnancy, women's fashions, violence or anything else that is on your mind. In fact, staying general may be helpful because it will allow you to ask your teen for more specifics. These answers

can illuminate much about your teen's life and the cultural within which (s)he lives.

Bonding through Pop Culture
Bonding with your teen through pop culture may seem like an impossible task, but all it takes is some time and effort from both sides. For example, asking all family members to engage in a once-a-month film night or beginning a discussion about favourite books while on a car journey will help you stay in touch with what your kids are seeing and doing. Sometimes getting a little silly or allowing your teens to laugh at you can help keep a conversation going. Play them some of your favourite teen songs or show them pictures of you in the height of fashion when you were a teenager. By building a bridge and showing them that you are interest in give-and-take, not just lecturing, you'll be more likely to keep your teen engaged.

Reiterating Family Values
When you are on the topic of pop culture is the prefect time to reiterate your family values. For example, discussing teen drinking gives you a great opening to remind teens that responsible drinking by those who are over the legal age is perfectly acceptable in your house, but that binge drinking and underage drinking is not. However, it is a fine line between simply stating your rules and lecturing them so be forewarned that teens may well tune out if they hear your tone change or suspect that you re going to tell them a list of things that are prohibited. Asking their opinion on matters, such as "That last film we saw was pretty gruesome. What did you think of the drug scenes?" will help keep them involved and show them that you think their thoughts and opinions are worthwhile. The more the two of you can interact the more you can both learn about pop culture and your family culture.

Pop culture and your teen can be a scary but exciting relationship. As a parent, watch how it develops and step in when you feel that it is needed. Good luck!

Teens need discipline. However, many parents fail to correct their children or provide boundaries. As a result, these young adults develop an "I can do whatever I want" attitude, and they do not respect other adults or authority. These youths are often defiant. Yet, there are ways to keep teens on the right path. Read on to learn how to discipline teens.

Make a few house rules. Teenagers need boundaries. Without limits, they're bound to run wild and get into trouble. Establish a reasonable curfew and assign household chores. Thus, they'll learn how to follow instructions and be responsible. Parents can include their teenagers in the decision and consider their input.

Establish punishments or consequences for bad actions. It's normal for teenagers to misbehave. Still, there ought to be consequences for repeated bad behavior. Take away their car keys, take the cellular phone or block their Internet access. Do whatever it takes to get their attention--they'll eventually get the point and adjust their attitude.

Be consistent with discipline. Some parents inconsistently discipline their teenagers. Teens respond well to regular correction. However, a few parents discipline when it's convenient for them. Enforce the rules every day, and follow through with punishments.

Stand your ground. Teenagers are strong-minded, and they know how to yell, manipulate and make hurtful remarks. Rather than shrink back, exercise authority and be the parent. This isn't the time to be a friend.

Control your anger. Teenagers can push parents to their limits. If necessary, leave the room and take a few minutes to calm down. Bad things can happen when anger surfaces.

Parents are often confused about how to deal with their teenagers. They are neither children, nor adults. They are seeking their individuality and independence and at the same time they are not really ready to be independent of their parents. Combine these emotions with raging hormones and you get a confused, rebellious individual. This is what makes dealing with and disciplining teenagers very difficult.

Chapter 18

How can you discipline your teen effectively?

• Make and enforce household rules. Make it clear to your teen that there are certain rules to be followed in your home. Let them know what is permitted and what is not, when they are expected to return after an outing, which friends are allowed to come home, what outfits are permitted and so on.
• Assign responsibilities to your teen. This shows that you trust them and they will be obliged to live up to it. Ask your teen to watch the younger kids or help you make meals. Such small and simple chores instil responsibility and a sense of worth in your children.
• Punish misdeeds. This will show your children that bad or improper actions won't be tolerated. However, punishments must be reasonable and related. There is no use asking your son to mow the lawn for the month because he scored poor grades. Instead ask him to refrain from going out with friends and participating in sports until he gets his grades up. Similarly, punishments should be practical. There is no use promising to ground your daughter for a lifetime if she gets home late. She knows that it is impossible. Instead make it clear to your daughter that her social life will come to a standstill if she cannot follow the rules and timings you have set for her.
• Discipline your teen consistently. Don't discipline your child only when you feel like it. They should know that bad deeds won't be tolerated even though you are busy or ill. Rules and punishments apply at all times.
• Don't let your teen manipulate you. Teens tend to do this. They may get angry and aggressive. Don't let this intimidate you. Stand firm in your decision so that your teen knows that

he won't be able to manipulate you. Alternately, your teen may use sentiments and tears to get their punishment reduced. Don't fall for such shows of emotion either.

• At times, let your child deal with the consequences of their actions. This applies only to certain circumstances. For example, you should not let your teen drive recklessly thinking that he ought to learn a lesson from the physical and financial consequences of a road accident. On the other hand if your teen scores bad grades, let him deal with the shame and resolve to score better.

• Spend time with your teen. Take time to talk to him or her and learn what is on their mind. Often, shows of anger and rebellion stem from underlying emotional turbulence. By understanding what is on your child's mind, you will be able to help them deal with their problems. Sometimes a parent has to become a friend if they want to get across to their teen.

• Never ever give in to violence or harsh words. Your teen may be testing your patience but by hurting them verbally or physically, you are only widening the gap between you and your child. If you find yourself getting angry, take some time to calm down before dealing with your teen

The following tips are for any parent who is worried about their child, or their own parenting skills:

You and your child

Make sure they know you love them and are proud of them. Even when things are busy or stressful, and it feels like you are in survival mode, a word or a hug can reassure them a huge amount. Praise them for what they do well, and encourage them to try new things

Be honest about your feelings – you don't have to be perfect. We all get things wrong and shout or say unkind things from time to time. If this happens, say sorry to your child afterwards and explain why it happened, They will learn from you that it's OK to make mistakes and that it doesn't make you a bad person

Be clear about what is and isn't acceptable – and tell them why. Children need to know what is OK and what isn't, and what will happen if they cross the line. Follow through on what you say as otherwise they may get confused or stop respecting the boundaries

Own your own role – you are the parent, so don't be afraid to take tough decisions. If your child sees you are scared of their reaction and always give in to them, it can make them feel very powerful, which can be frightening. Children need to know that you are there to keep them safe.

Helping your child

Worrying or difficult behaviour might be short-lived, so give it some time. All children go through stages of feeling anxious or angry and they can show this in lots of ways, for example, tantrums, crying, sleeping problems or fighting with friends or siblings. They might be adapting to a change in the family or in their school life, or just trying out new emotions, and will generally grow out of worrying behaviour on their own or with family support

Talk to your child: Even young children can understand about feelings and behaviour if you give them a chance to talk about it. Take it gently and give them examples of what you mean, for example, 'When you said you hated Molly, you looked really angry. What was making you so cross?' or 'When you can't get to sleep, is there anything in your mind making you worried?'

With older children, they might not want to talk at first. Let them know you are concerned about them, and are there if they need you. Sending an email or a text can work better if this is the way your child likes to communicate

Ask your child what they think would help – they often have good ideas about solving their own problems

If you can, talk to your child's other parent about your worries, when the child is not around. They might have a different take on what's going on. Try and sort out how to deal with the behaviour together so you are using the same approach, and can back each other up. Children are quick to spot if parents disagree, and can try and use this to get their own way

More advice on when to think about getting professional help, and what to do, if you are concerned about your child's behaviour.

Looking after yourself

If your child is having problems, don't be too hard on yourself or blame yourself. Although it can be upsetting and worrying if your child is having a bad time, and it makes your relationship with them feels more stressful, you are not a bad parent. Children often take it out on those closest to them, so you might be feeling the effect of their very powerful emotions

If you had a difficult time growing up yourself, or have had emotional problems or mental health problems, it can be very worrying to think that the same thing might happen to your child. But the love and care you show them and the fact that you are trying to help will protect against this. Getting help for them and perhaps for yourself too can give them the best chance of feeling better

If things are getting you down, it's important to recognise this. Talk to someone you trust and see what they think. Many people go on struggling with very difficult situations because they feel they should be able to cope, and don't deserve any help

Friends and family can often help – don't be afraid to ask them to have your child for a bit if you need some time out to sort out your own stuff. You can repay them when things get better for you!

It's easy to say take some time for yourself but in reality this may not feel possible. You might be too busy, exhausted or hard up for exercise or hobbies. But even a night in with a friend, a DVD box set or your favourite dinner can help Go to your GP if things are really getting on top of you. Asking for some support from your doctor or a referral to a counselling service is a sign of strength. You can't help your child if you are not being supported yourself. Some people worry their parenting will be judged and their children will be taken away if they admit they are struggling to cope. This should only happen if a child is being abused or neglected and the role of professionals is to support you to look after your child as well as you can.

Pointers for the future
 It is important to recognise and encourage positive behaviour and to deal with and challenge negative behaviour, deal with it to a satisfactory conclusion and then move on. As adults we tend to bring things back from the past into the present but it is important to understand that young people's thoughts are in the here and now i.e. in the present.

Discipline- You both need to set out boundaries and guidelines and make sure you stick to them, without negotiation, after a full explanation has been given. After an explanation has been given do not bring up the issue again at that time. You need to let them know how their behaviour and actions make you feel without using physical or verbal aggression.

If you wouldn't accept the behaviour from a stranger then there would be no reason to accept the behaviour from your child.

"No" means "No" therefore give an explanation and keep to it without negotiation. Relate to them in the Adult-to-Adult role.

If needed, challenge them on their language and behaviour with explanations and reasons and let them take responsibility, in a positive way, by doing things for themselves they will build up the trust they want to rebuild.

It is my feeling that if challenges are not created for them, they will become involved in negative
Expectations and consequences must be spelled out ahead of time in order for them to be most effective. Both the child and the parent must know exactly what behavior is expected and what consequences will follow.
There are three general ways that this can be accomplished.

Use Natural Consequences

Some behaviours carry with them natural consequences, and these consequences are often sufficient to produce change and a good way to start. A few examples follow.

"I serve supper between 5:00 and 6:00 P.M. The kitchen closes at 6:00." The child who comes home at 6:30 is faced with the natural consequence of not eating or of preparing his own meal.

"I only wash clothes that are placed in the hamper." The natural consequences of not putting clothes where they belong are that you cannot wear them, you wash them yourself, or you wear them dirty.

"I am giving you your allowance on Friday. This is supposed to last until next Friday. I will not give you any more money until then." The natural consequences of going out Friday night and spending your entire allowance is that you will not have any money for the remainder of the week.

"Anyone who breaks something in the house will be responsible for paying for the repair." The natural consequence of slamming a door and breaking it is that the person who slammed it will have to come up with the money to pay for it.

The natural consequence that I frequently use in dealing with the teenager centres on cooperation in the home. In other words, the parent is telling the child, "If you cooperate with me, I'll cooperate with you. Everyone here has certain chores and responsibilities. If I have to pick up after you because you fail to do your job, I will have to use some of my free time to do what you were supposed to do. Therefore, I will not have time to do what you want."

Many teenagers feel that their parents are always on their back, asking them to do too many things. They complain, "I wish my parents would leave me alone and let me do what *I* want." Some teenagers feel as though they do ten things for their parents for every one thing the parents do for them. Frequently, natural consequences are used to deal with this situation. The parent might tell the child, "You don't want me to ask you to do things, and you want me to quit hassling you. Well, I'll be more than happy to do this, but, remember, if I don't ask you to do things for me, you can't ask me to do things for you." At first the child thinks this is a good deal. But after a while she realizes that she is getting the short end of the deal and that the parent does more for her than she realized.

Many approaches to teenage behavior stress natural or logical consequences as methods of dealing with it. However, two things must be kept in mind when using natural consequences. First, the natural consequence has to be important to the child in order for it to be effective. For example, the natural consequence of telling a teenager "I will not wash any of your clothes that are not put in the clothes hamper" will not work effectively for a child who does not care whether he wears clean or dirty outfits.

The other thing to consider before using this technique is whether you want the natural consequence to occur. One morning at 4:00 A.M. I got a call from a very upset mother. She told me that her 13-year-old son had left the house at seven o'clock the previous evening and was not yet home. When I asked what had happened, she told me that the boy and his father had had an argument about cleaning his room. When the child refused, the father responded angrily, "This is my house and as long as you live here you have to do what I want you to do, and I am telling you to clean your room!" After quite a bit of arguing, the father eventually warned, "If you don't like the rules in this house, you can leave," and the child left. The child experienced the natural consequence in this situation, but of course the parents did not want this to be the outcome.

In using this technique, parents must respond in a very matter-of-fact manner. You should try not to become upset, shout, or carry on. You have to be sure that the consequence is important to the child and you must consistently follow through with what is said.

Use Grandma's Rule

This is a principle that most parents can use frequently. It can be stated very simply as, "You do what I want you to do and then you can do what you want to do." Or, "You do what I want you to do and then I'll do what you want me to do." Similarly, your mother may have promised, "Eat your meat and potatoes, and then you can have your dessert." Natural consequences are things that are built into the environment, whereas this method of setting consequences can be ad-libbed and used on the spur of the moment.

Use Important Consequences

When either natural consequences or Grandma's Rule cannot be used, you should try to identify consequences that are important to the child and to set the rules of behavioural expectations according to these. The consequences can be positive - things that do not happen every day at your house (extra phone time, staying out late, or having a friend sleep over). They can also be negative (loss of privileges, grounding and restrictions). Any privilege, activity, or request that is important to the child can serve as a consequence of his behavior.

The child who wants to stay out later on the weekend may earn this privilege through more involvement in schoolwork during the week.

Extra phone time or having a friend sleep over may be earned by a child who makes an effort to get along better with his siblings.

An allowance could be earned by doing chores.

Positive consequences like the above enable a child to obtain a privilege or have a request granted.

Another method of using important consequences would be to set up situations where the teenager is being restricted or is losing particular privileges by behaving in certain ways.

The child who talks back to his parents may not get the new tennis shoes he wanted.

The teenager who does not come home on time on Friday night may lose the right to go out on Saturday night.

In all of these examples, we identify a consequence that is important to the child and then set the behavioural expectations according to this. It is not a natural consequence or something that automatically follows an activity, but it is a consequence that parents can create and individualize according to the interests, desires, and wishes of the particular adolescent.

Using Consequences to Change Behaviour

Consequences are the most important aspects of behavior management. They are the primary determinates of whether a child will change his behavior and develop new behaviours. A child must consistently experience consequences in order to change.

The range of consequences that can be used dramatically decreases as the youngster enters adolescence. The nine-year-old will respond to numerous consequences. When this same child becomes 13, the number of important consequences starts decreasing, and oftentimes the range is very small. For the teenager, many of the important consequences centre around money, cars, telephone, clothing, driving privileges, going out, more freedom, loosening of restrictions, and being treated like an adult. If the adolescent has a hobby (e.g., fishing, music), the range of important consequences may somewhat increase.

There are three major consequences that parents can use in dealing with their teenagers:

Rewards, incentives, or positive consequences. If you see a behavior you like, reward it; that is, follow the behavior with some positive attention and something that is important or enjoyable to the child.

Punishment or negative consequences. If you see a behavior you do not like, punish it; that is, follow the behavior with negative attention and something the child views as not enjoyable, or withdraw something positive.

Ignoring or no consequences. If you see a behavior you do not like, ignore it because maybe the attention you pay to it is the reason it exists. In other words, do not follow the behavior with either negative or positive attention.

Reward, punishment, and ignoring are the three major consequences that can be used in disciplining teenagers.

Chapter 19

What Is Oppositional Defiant Disorder?

Oppositional defiant disorder is a behavioural disorder diagnosed in children and teens. Teens with ODD are, as the name suggests, oppositional and defiant toward authority figures, including their parents. According to the American Psychiatric Association, these teens will exhibit behaviours that include often losing their temper, arguing with adults, defying or refusing to comply with rules, purposefully annoying other people and blaming others for their mistakes or misdeeds. In addition, they are often touchy, annoyed, angry, resentful, spiteful or vindictive. To be diagnosed with ODD, these behaviours must have been present for six months and must have caused problems for the teen at school, with peers, at work or at home.

ODD and Other Disorders

Diagnosing and treating ODD can be difficult because, as the American Academy of Child and Adolescent Psychiatry, or AACAP, points out, ODD often co-occurs with other mental disorders. It is especially common among teens with attention-deficit hyperactivity disorder, or ADHD. It also commonly co-occurs with obsessive compulsive disorder and mood disorders such a major depression, anxiety disorder and bipolar disorder. According to the Substance Abuse and Mental Health Services Administration, or SAMHSA, teens with ODD may go on to develop a similar behavioural disorder known as conduct disorder, which is characterized by actively aggressive, destructive and illegal acts. However, teens cannot carry a diagnosis of ODD and conduct disorder at the same time.

Causes

The cause of ODD is not known. According to the AACAP, the disorder may originate in combative parent-child behavioural patterns established early in childhood. S. Sutton Hamilton, M.D., and John Armando, L.C.S.W., writing in the American Family Physician journal, suggest that the disorder may result from a cognitive deficit that causes the teen to become overwhelmed and react emotionally to simple requests and demands from authority figures.

Parent Training Programs

Among the primary treatments for ODD are parent training programs. As described by the AACAP, these classes provide parents with practical advice and techniques for managing their defiant teens. "Parents are taught negotiating skills, techniques of positive reinforcement, and other means of reducing the power struggles and establishing more effective and consistent discipline."

Therapy

Various types of therapy are also effective at helping teens with ODD and their families, the AACAP reports. In individual psychotherapy, the therapist can help the teen explore his feelings and develop anger management strategies. Cognitive-behavioural therapy techniques can help teens develop problem-solving skills in order to effectively handle situations that may otherwise overwhelm them. In family therapy, the therapist can involve the whole family at once in order to address dysfunctional family dynamics and improve interfamily communication.

Medication

Medications are only used in teens with OCD who have co-occurring mental disorders such as ADHD, obsessive-compulsive disorder or anxiety disorder, Hamilton and Armando report. Several studies have shown that patients with both ODD and ADHD who are treated with ADHD medications such as Ritalin, Adderall or Strattera experience improvement in their symptoms of ODD. However, a study led by Mark E. Bangs, M.D., and published in the journal Paediatrics in 2008, reported that one such drug, Strattera, had no beneficial effects on ODD symptoms.

Defiance may seem to court your adolescent with the same fervour of the paparazzi stalking stars at a celebrity function. It can start slowly with shrugs over questions about homework and grow into outright refusal to turn the television off, clean his bedroom or honour a curfew. But your teen's defiance is likely normal, and a common sense approach to discipline can help parents and teens through this temporary phase of adolescence.

Normal Teen Defiance

The moodiness, self-absorption and preoccupation your teen has with his peer group may make you question your parenting ability. But mental health professionals at the American Academy of Child and Adolescent Psychiatry report that all teens, including the healthy, well-balanced ones, sometimes become argumentative, belligerent and defiant. They note that even your reasonable requests that he clean his room or empty the dishwasher can result in passive resistance or a sudden tirade over what he sees as rigid, impossible or ridiculous rules.

Causes

Well-documented hormonal fluctuations and the natural need to gain independence during puberty can bring the swift swings in mood and defiance so often related to adolescence. Along with that, however, Dr. Andrew Garner of the American Academy of Paediatrics notes that natural brain development may cause some of your teen's oppositional defiance. During an interview for Healthy Children magazine, Garner noted that the parts of the brain that regulate the ability to look ahead and see the consequences of behavior do not reach maturity until late adolescence or young adulthood. But the part of the brain that regulates emotion and reflexive responses develops fully during early adolescence. Scientists believe this mismatch in brain development may cause teens to behave impulsively despite knowing better.

Disciplining Your Defiant Teen

Noting that discipline is as important for teens as preschoolers, the Kids Health website recommends that you continue to define and enforce rules for your adolescent. The website suggests discussing and clarifying your expectations about homework, curfews and dating. But teens need to have some participation in laying the groundwork. For instance, Kids Health suggests that you allow your teen to choose his hairstyle, clothing and room decorations, but set limits on issues such as curfew based on age and maturity. Taking away privileges, such as restricting driving for a specified time, might work best for disciplining teenagers. Discussing the reasons why missing curfew and other discipline problems worry parents might keep tempers from flaring too hotly when you do suspend his driving privileges.

Prevention/Solution

Parents cannot expect to prevent all teenage defiance any more than you would expect a 1-year-old to walk gracefully during his first attempt to toddle across the room. But staying calm during the outbursts, refusing to argue over agreed-upon limits and remembering that he is likely as confused as you over his feelings can help prevent battles from becoming war. Kids Health also suggests that you periodically review your parenting style to make sure you allow him to think independently and develop tastes that might differ from your own. Pick your battles wisely. For instance, allow him to choose a different political party than yours, but enforce the rules if he opts for an afternoon at the beach instead of school.

Considerations

The American Academy of Child and Adolescent Psychiatry notes that a pattern of extreme defiance or hostile behavior toward authority that interferes with a teenager's daily functioning may signal something more serious than normal teenage angst. Oppositional defiant disorder or conduct disorder generally require behavior management training and help with problem-solving skills. If you believe your teen has a behavioural disorder, see your family physician for recommendations and referrals regarding evaluation and treatment.

Autism is a developmental disorder that affects communication, relationships and behavior. Although researchers have found evidence that autism begins before birth, and signs appear during infancy as the young person matures, the challenges of adolescence can cause new signs to emerge.

The goal of the teen years is to prepare for launch into independent adult life, while simultaneously forming community. Working towards these goals is important and more challenging for the autistic teen.

Communication Difficulties

Some autistic teens have very limited interactive communication, according to the National Institute of Neurological Disorders and Stroke. They repeat phrases they hear, a pattern called echolia, or say the same words over and over again, enjoying the sounds and familiarity of them. Other young adults can engage in conversations, but may have trouble initiating discussions or maintaining interest in what the other person is saying.

Inflexibility

When any child feels unsafe or anxious, he can fall back on familiar rituals or routines that provide comfort. For the autistic teen, this can be more exaggerated, and the source of the discomfort may not be obvious from the outside. In school, the normal amount of pressure associated with homework and moving from class to class through crowded hallways can be the stimulus for the teen to withdrawal into the safe harbour of his ritualistic behavior. Some teens find a small school to be more manageable, and others make time in their schedules to be by themselves and regroup emotionally between classes. What's important is that strategies, which can be used in the workplace as an adult, are nurtured during the high school years.

Advanced Vocabulary in Narrowed Areas of Interest

Adolescents with autism may have developed sophisticated vocabularies in relation to their one or two areas of intense interest, and may be able to discuss those areas more fluidly than they could as children. The American Academy of Child and Adolescent Psychiatry notes that preoccupation on a very narrow area of interest is also indicative of Asperger's Syndrome, a related disorder on the autism spectrum.

Poor Perception of Risk and Pain

Autistic teens may underestimate or be oblivious to risks or pain, or they may exaggerate them. In childhood, parents can watch for danger, but in the teen years, any move towards independence involves accepting an inherent increase in risk. Shana Nichols, the author of "Girls Growing Up on the Autism Spectrum" notes that young women with autism may be at risk of sexual dangers, including unwanted sexual activity, sexually transmitted diseases and HIV-AIDS, and teen pregnancy, because they look as if they are capable of consenting, but they don't fully understand the risks involved. Driving is possible for some teens with autism, but a correct perception of danger and the ability to sustain concentration must be in place first.

Depression

There is a physical basis for depression in some autistic teens and a social one, as well. Seizure disorders occur more frequently in autistic individuals, with 20 to 30 percent developing epilepsy by early adulthood, according to the National Institutes of Neurological Disorders and Stroke, and seizure disorders are closely linked to depression. In addition, teens with autism face many moments of social rejection, and the differences between their own lives and those of the people they see around them become more obvious as they approach high school graduation and this, too, can cause depression.

Chapter 20

ADHD

While some ADHD symptoms disappear by adolescence, as many as 80 percent of ADHD kids will continue to display symptoms as teens, according to Dr. David Goodman, Assistant Professor of Psychiatry and Behavioural Sciences at Johns Hopkins University. Many mental health professionals follow a multimodal approach that utilizes several different treatment options that when combined successfully meet the individual needs of each teen.

Medications

There are a variety of stimulant medications designed to enhance focus and reduce ADHD-related impulse control and hyperactivity, according to the Kids Health website. Stimulant medications include methylphenidate (Ritalin), dextroamphetamine (Dexedrine), and pemoline (Cylert). Side effects can include difficulty sleeping and reduced appetite. While stimulants remain the first-line of treatment from a medication standpoint, non-stimulant medications may work when patients cannot tolerate the side effects of stimulants. Common non-stimulant medications include those also used to treat high blood pressure and depression. Examples include atomoxetine (Strattera) bupropion (Wellbutrin), fluoxetine (Prozac), guanfacine (Tenex), imipramine (Tofranil), nortriptyline (Pamelor), and sertraline (Zoloft). Many of these are not as effective at treating hyperactivity, and also have a variety of side effects, according to the Help Guide website.

According to a 2004 study conducted for the National Mental Health Association, nearly nine in ten parents with an ADHD teen believe prescription medication is the most effective treatment for ADHD.

Individual Therapy

Individual therapy helps teach coping skills, while providing an educational background about the condition, according to the Kids Health website. Therapy can take many forms, according to the American Academy of Child and Adolescent Psychiatry (AACAP). During cognitive behavioural sessions, teens learn to modify social behaviours, which can include problem-solving strategies for controlling their bodies and focusing their attention.

Social skills training uses reinforcement strategies that reward appropriate behavior, ultimately teaching teens to evaluate a social situation and adjust their behavior accordingly. The AACAP website points out that when coupled with cognitive therapy and medication, social skills training helps teens to smooth out awkward or difficult social behaviours that often accompany other ADHD symptoms.

Family Counselling

Family counselling and parent training programs are helpful when dealing with an ADHD teen, according to the Kids Health website. These programs provide ADHD education to all members of the family, while providing parents with often much needed parenting strategies. Parents learn negotiating skills and positive reinforcement techniques to help manage a teen's ADHD behavior.

Teenagers who struggle with attention-deficit hyperactivity disorder (ADHD) have a harder time being successful at school and making and maintaining relationships with peers. The disorder is characterized by impulsivity, hyperactivity and inattention. Teens are impulsive by nature, so when a teen has this disorder, impulsivity can result in dangerous behaviours such as using drugs and having unprotected sex, without thinking about the consequences. It's important that teens with this disorder receive treatment to reduce their symptoms.

Basics

Each teen responds differently to specific medications. One teen might find a good fit on the first try, but more than likely, it will take time to find the right medication or combination of medications to treat the disorder. Doctors usually start a teen off on a small dose and increase the dosage over time in order to deal with any negative side effects that arise.

Common Medications

After your teen receives a diagnosis of ADHD from a mental health professional, medication may be recommended to help alleviate the symptoms that make it hard for your teen to concentrate in school, relate to his peers and make well-thought-out decisions. According to the National Institute of Mental Health, the most common form of medication used to treat this disorder in all age groups is stimulants. Some common stimulants include Ritalin, Adderall and Dexedrine. These medications come in different forms, such as pills, skin patches and liquids. They also come in short-acting, long-acting and extended-release varieties.

Types of Therapy

Another form of treatment for teen ADHD is therapy, which also comes in different forms. Individual therapy, social skills training, family therapy and group therapy can be used to treat this mental health issue in adolescents. The most common type of individual therapy used to treat ADHD is cognitive behavioural therapy, which helps an adolescent understand how her thoughts affect her emotions and behaviours.

Family therapy is usually an important piece of treatment with children and teens, because everyone in the family is impacted by the disorder. In family therapy, parents learn the symptoms, the impact of the symptoms and different types of treatment. The family practices effective methods of communication and parents are taught how to deal with specific situations.

Lifestyle Changes

Therapists and doctors will also work with teens and their families in incorporating healthy lifestyle changes in order to reduce the symptoms of ADHD. It's important that a teen with this disorder get at least eight hours of sleep each night, eat healthfully and get regular exercise. A therapist might suggest that a teen join a team sport at school to practice social skills and reduce the symptoms of hyperactivity. Learning time management skills and communication skills can also help teens cope with this disorder.

Considerations

Teens that have coexisting disorders such as a mood disorder or an anxiety disorder will need more intensive forms of treatment and may require different types of medication. Adolescents that have coexisting substance abuse issues will need treatment that addresses both mental health problems. Children, teens and adults who struggle with attention-deficit hyperactivity disorder (ADHD) can use behavioural strategies to reduce the symptoms of impulsivity, inattention and hyperactivity. Behavioural strategies are a big component of cognitive-behavioural therapy which is used to treat ADHD in all age groups. Many times, cognitive-behavioural therapists assign behavioural techniques as homework.

Regular Exercise and Sleep

It's extremely important that people with ADHD---no matter their ages---exercise regularly and get a good night's sleep each night, according to Helpguide.org. Parents who have a child with this disorder should encourage their child to join team sports, play outdoors and get moving daily. This will help decrease hyperactivity and increase attention. Sleep also improves the ability to concentrate.

Routine

While all people with ADHD benefit from having a specific routine, this is especially true for children. Nicole Sprinkle from ADDitude magazine reports that children with this disorder need structure, but they shouldn't be the only family members with a daily routine. Plans should include a routine for all children in the family. Parents should incorporate into the daily routine times that children wake up, eat breakfast, eat lunch, do homework, eat dinner and go to bed. Try to follow the routine even when the children don't have school.

Lists and Planners

A behavioural strategy that teens and adults with this disorder should implement is keeping a planner with daily lists of tasks to complete, according to the Mayo Clinic. It's helpful to write out tasks for the next day before bed and cross them off as they're finished throughout the day. People with ADHD struggle with remembering important dates and appointments, so they can benefit from writing all of them down in a planner and reviewing the planner on a regular basis.

Break Down Large Tasks

Children, teens and adults with ADHD become overwhelmed by large tasks. They often get distracted and the tasks often don't get finished. The Mayo Clinic recommends breaking down large tasks into smaller tasks that are more manageable. Parents of children with ADHD can assist them in doing this. For instance, if a child has to complete a science project, the parents can help the child break it down into tasks that will take about 20 to 30 minutes each to complete, assigning each task to specific days.

Get Organized

Almost everyone with ADHD struggles with organization. Many times, therapists will suggest behavioural strategies to reduce disorganization. For instance, a therapist might recommend that the client pick one room in her house each week to organize. After the house is organized, the therapist might suggest that the client pick up trash, loose papers and anything else out of place for 10 minutes each evening.

Most of the information written about adolescents and teenagers places a great deal of emphasis on the physical, social, and emotional changes, accompanied by confusion and uncertainty, which mark this developmental stage of a child's life. While it is certainly a difficult period for the child, it is likewise true that the parents are also experiencing stresses, changes, and confusion at this time. Not much has been written about the parents' problems and worries, as well as the changes they are undergoing as they approach midlife with a teenager in their household.

It is important to recognize some of the normal behaviours and reactions of parents and teens during this period. Many parents perceive certain teen attitudes and behaviours to be problems, whereas in reality these may follow typical adolescent patterns and should be dealt with as such. Following are some suggestions on how to distinguish between normal and abnormal behavior in an adolescent, and how to decide whether the behavior should be of no concern, or of mild, moderate, or great concern to the parent.

Chapter 21

What Is Normal?

How moody should a child be? How talkative, rebellious, oppositional, or resistant? What is normal teenage behavior? These questions are difficult to answer specifically. In general, normal behavior is behavior that does not interfere with a person's ability to cope with his environment or to get along with others. It is relatively easy to find a child-development book that will tell you at what age a child should walk, talk, or get his or her first tooth. Other books will tell you what to expect at certain ages (e.g., the "terrible twos"). But just how do you determine what is a normal amount of flippancy or moodiness in your teenager? In trying to decide what is typical, there are several factors to consider.

Become Aware of the Attitudes and Behaviours of Adolescents Your Child's Age

I am not recommending that you keep up with the Joneses or go along with the crowd. However, you must consider your teenager's peer group and take into account the behaviours and actions of his age mates in order to determine if your teenager's behavior is typical or should be of concern. In other words, you have to compare your child with other children his age. Talk to other parents with teenagers. Observe your child's friends and other similar-age children.

The child's peer groups - their behaviours, attitudes, dress, and values - must be taken into consideration before deciding what is normal for your child. But, you also must try to determine what the "normal" peer groups are. Some peer groups are themselves deviant, and may be associated with serious impairments or difficulties.

Teachers, coaches, tutors, dance instructors, school counsellors, and others who work with teenagers are usually familiar with age-appropriate or normal behavior. Although they may not be able to give reasons for certain behavior or recommendations for dealing with it, they can identify actions differing from those of the child's age group.

How Often Does the Behaviour Occur?

All children, at one time or another, are moody, argumentative, or withdrawn. However, to determine if the behavior or attitude is cause for concern, it is important to note its frequency. A child who is occasionally flip or insolent is certainly not that unusual, compared to a child who is fresh every time she talks to her parents. The more frequently the behavior is seen, the more it may deviate from normal.

Does the Behaviour Interfere with the Teenager's Ability to Function in the Environment?

All of us become depressed at times, but if this feeling or attitude prevents us from going to work or completing necessary duties around the house, then it should be a concern. If it does not significantly interfere with our daily functioning, however, then concern about this attitude and behavior can be somewhat minimized. Similarly, most children share an aversion to homework and some also to class work, but if this attitude or behavior results in failing grades or the necessity to attend summer school, then it may be considered not typical and should be a concern. If it does not restrict or prevent the teen from functioning like an average child, however, then parents need have less concern.

Does the Behaviour Interfere with Others?

Most siblings occasionally fight with one another, but if this type of behavior on the part of one child provokes a fearful or negative reaction on the part of the sibling, it may not be considered normal. A teenager who always fights with a younger sibling can disrupt the household from the time he comes home from school until the time he goes to bed. Conduct that significantly interferes with the routines, behaviours, and activities of other members of the household may deviate from the norm and be of concern.

Consider Individual Differences

Children have different personalities. One child may be sensitive, another talkative, a third shy, and so forth. In determining whether behavior is normal, you have to consider not only the teenager's peer group, but also the individual child. For example, a teenager who has never been very talkative and who tends to bottle up her emotions may display this behavior to a higher degree when she reaches adolescence. A stubborn, strong-willed child may show more rebellion during adolescence than one who is compliant and passive.

In general, in trying to determine whether a behavior is normal or should be of concern, you can ask the following questions. How different is the behavior or attitude when compared with other children in her age group or her normal personality? How frequently does it occur? Does it interfere with others or with your child's ability to cope with her environment or to get along with people (not only her parents, but teachers, coaches, friends, neighbours, and others whom she deals with on a daily basis)?

Many teenagers who have trouble with trust and responsibility are similar to the "behavior kids"; in order to develop self-discipline and a responsible attitude, they must first develop the desired behavior (cleaning their room, doing their homework, coming home on time). In other words, the focus is more on behavior than on attitude. After the behavior is developed, hopefully an appropriate attitude will gradually be established. The following techniques help the child develop self-discipline, responsibility, and trust.

Define the Rule and the Consequence

You must tell the teenager what you expect, but more important than the rule is what will happen if she complies with your request and what will happen if she does not. Spell out rules and consequences at the same time. Put the responsibility onto the adolescent's shoulders. If good things happen to her, it is up to her. If bad things happen, it is also up to her.

The general techniques of setting rules and consequences are discussed in detail in another section. I would suggest that you review this information, because these rules are the primary techniques that are used to develop responsible behaviours. When trying to develop responsibility in youngsters, many parents focus primarily on assigning chores (cutting grass, putting out the garbage, feeding the dog). This is fine, but it is not the main way that children develop responsible behavior. Chores usually involve consequences; that is, if a child does not put out the garbage, he does not get his allowance. The reason that chores are often used to develop responsibility is that predictable consequences usually follow the teenager's behavior. Therefore, when you are trying to develop responsibility or self-discipline in your child, you should spell out the rule and the consequence before the rule is broken. Then whatever happens to the teenager is a result of his behavior and no one else's. Responsible behavior can be encouraged throughout the day with this method.

Also, by spelling out consequences ahead of time, you avoid using random discipline and giving the teenager the impression that others are responsible for the consequence that has happened to him. This is extremely important to the adolescent, because with random discipline he feels unfairly treated. Most parents are careful and specific rule setters: "I want you home at 1:00 A.M., no later." However, many parents make the mistake of deciding the consequence after the teenager breaks the rule. Under these circumstances, the youngster is apt to feel unjustly treated. If an adolescent is dealt with primarily in this fashion, it is somewhat difficult for him to feel in control of what happens to him and to develop responsibility for his own behavior.

Tie All Consequences to the Child's Behaviour

At first when trying to develop responsibility in some teenagers, it is best to tie as many consequences as possible to their behavior. In other words, you set up a situation where the adolescents will earn their rewards and pleasures, as well as their punishments and disappointments. Not only do you spell out disciplinary measures ahead of time, but you also try to relate all consequences to their behavior. Put them in control of the consequences of their actions - good or bad. Tell the teenager who has been using the phone every night but doing nothing around the house that she now has to earn this privilege by performing some chore.

Set up a rule and a consequence for your son so that he no longer gets to use the car on weekends unless he shows you certain behaviours.

Inform your daughter, who used to get on the Internet just for breathing, that she now has to perform certain duties in order to have access to the computer.

Avoid Assuming Responsibility

You should not assume responsibility for the teenager or her behavior. Make her responsible. If you force her to do her homework every night or do it for her, you are more responsible for the work being completed than the child. If you have to tell your son 47 times to take out the garbage before he complies, you are more responsible for the task than the child is. And the next night you will probably have to do the same thing. The teenager completes the task, but he doesn't develop responsibility or independent behavior. You may have to act as his motivator until he gets married or leaves the house.

For days a parent tells her child to clean his room, but it never gets done. Eventually, she gets fed up, drags him to the room, stands over him, and makes him clean it. In several minutes the room is spotless, but who is responsible for the room being cleaned?

The parent. A better way to get this room cleaned and encourage responsibility in the teenager would be to spell out expectations and consequences ahead of time. Put the responsibility on the adolescent. Avoid forcing him to do what he is supposed to do.

These same situations occur when parents allow a teenager to become dependent on them. Either the parents help the teenager excessively, or they do things for her. This may involve picking up after teens, keeping their rooms cleaned, waking them up for school, locating their keys. When parents act in this way, the adolescent finds it difficult to learn independent and responsible behaviours because it is easier to let someone else do things for her. Avoid allowing the teenager to become too dependent on you for performing tasks for her that she is physically capable of doing. Children who are spoiled and often have their needs met for them, who are in more control than their parents, or who frequently get their own way also have a difficult time developing responsible behaviours. The same situation exists when parents "run interference" for the teenager and protect him from experiencing the consequences of his actions. This parent-child interaction should be avoided to establish self-discipline and responsibility.

Make the Consequences Different for Positive and for Negative Behaviours

Some teenagers do not develop responsible behaviours because the same thing happens to them whether they perform the required task or not. The adolescent thinks, "I'll be able to go out Friday night whether or not I cooperate around the house" or "I'll be able to use the computer whether or not I do my homework." If someone said to me, "You can go to work and I will pay you, or you can stay home and I will pay you," I certainly would be out fishing instead of working. In fact, I would have to be stupid to go to work. The same situation exists for children who feel that if they get into a jam, they will be able to manipulate their way out of the situation and again they will not experience the consequences. You have to make the consequences different for teenagers if you expect to change their behavior or develop an attitude of responsibility. In other words, one thing will happen if the adolescent cooperates around the house and something entirely different will happen if he does not cooperate. Be sure the teenager is experiencing different consequences for different behaviours.

Win the War and Forget About the Battles

Sometimes it is better to lose a few battles, but win the war. It may be more important for your teenager to experience the consequences of his behavior than it would be for you to get the task accomplished. For example, you say, "You cannot leave the house today until you clean the fish tank." He comes back with, "I don't care. I didn't want to go anywhere. I'm going in the den to watch television." Now you think, "What am I going to do now?" The answer is "Nothing." The rule sticks. In this example, getting the fish tank cleaned should be actually the fourth thing you are trying to accomplish. The first thing is to make the teenager aware that there will be two different consequences to his behavior, positive and negative. The second thing you are trying to achieve is to teach the child that he is responsible for his behavior. In other words, "Whether you go out in two minutes, two hours, two days, or two weeks, there is only one person in the entire world who can determine that and that is you. You are responsible for what happens to you." The third thing is to teach him: "I am going to do what you tell me to do. I am going to consistently follow through with the consequences that you decide. The consequences that happen to you depend totally on your actions. If you do not clean the fish tank, you are telling me that you do not want to leave the house and I am going to be sure that this happens. If you clean the tank, you are telling me that you want to go outside and I will follow through with that."

Sometimes, parents continually battle with a teenager - about homework, cleaning up the bathroom, picking up clothes, cleaning up after herself. They try to win each battle by forcing the child to do what they request. Although they eventually win each battle, the teenager does not develop any independent or responsible behavior. Your daughter refuses to help in the kitchen and you tell her, "If you do not help me, I will not be able to pick up your boyfriend after school tomorrow and bring him to the house. If you help me, I will be able to bring him." Now perhaps the child will refuse to help you in the kitchen and not have you pick up her boyfriend. You may look at this as, "I lost. She won." However, it is more important that she experience the consequences of not cooperating than that you force her to help. After this happens a few times, she may be more responsive when you say, "Would you please help me in the kitchen?" For some behaviour, it may not be important to get the child to comply. When the teenager experiences the consequences of her behavior today, you may get more cooperation tomorrow. Most times you can forget about the battles and focus on the war.

Do not get into power struggles if the teenager refuses to cooperate. You are dealing with a young adult and must exert a different form of control than used with the younger child. A parent tells a teenager to do something, he refuses and then an argument starts and develops into a power struggle. Avoid this scenario whenever possible and deal with your teen calmly.

Maintain a Businesslike Approach

Some people will do things for you because of a relationship that has been formed or because you have been nice to them. Other people would see this willingness as a weakness that can be exploited and used. Suppose you have done ten favours for me in the past. One morning you ask me to drive you to pick up your car, which has been repaired. I am busy and do not want to take you, but ten flags pop up in my head and remind me of the favours that you have done for me and the fact that you have been very nice to me. Therefore, I say, "Come on, I'll take you. Where do we have to go?" Another personality type might think that he has "put something over" on the person ten times and say, "No, I can't take you. I am busy." Some people you can pay in advance to paint your house, and you know the work will be completed. Others you would never pay until the job is finished; otherwise, it might never be completed. Most business contracts have rules that must be followed in order for the contract to be fulfilled. Never tell the teenager, "I am going to get you a new fishing rod, and because I've gotten it for you, I want you to improve in school." It is better to say "We can get your new fishing rod as soon as you improve in school." The child needs rules or expectations and consequences spelled out ahead of time, and consequences should occur after she fulfils the expectation, not before. "You promised to cut the grass this afternoon. You will get your allowance after the grass is cut, not before."

Avoid Harsh, Lengthy, or Major Consequences

Some teenagers learn responsibility by repetition of consequences. For them, rather than have one big thing happen, it would be better if they experience twenty small consequences. Rather than taking away the phone for a month at a time, it might be better to take it away twenty times for one day. Severe, harsh, or lengthy punishments usually will work with the "attitude kid." For example, if you took away her phone privileges for a month, the attitude kid would go to her room every afternoon and think, "What a stupid thing I did. I can't talk to my friends. It's boring not to be able to talk on the phone." In other words, you would get her thinking about what she had done and the consequences she is experiencing. Using this approach with "attitude kids" can help to change their thinking pattern or to develop a new attitude. On the other hand, the "behavior kid" would miss the phone for the first day or two, then adapt to the situation and not talk on the phone or go down to the corner convenience store and use that phone.

Major, lengthy, or harsh consequences do not affect some teenagers. So failing a grade or having to go to summer school may not significantly change a behavior. Although a child may have to go to summer school, he nevertheless escapes doing homework dozens of times, and the major consequence of failing or going to summer school will not change his attitude about homework. It's better for this personality type to have the parent check with the teacher every Friday, and if the boy has completed all of his homework and class work, positive consequences follow. If he has not completed the work, a different consequence occurs. Using this approach a number of times a year is more effective than imposing one large consequence.

A "behaviour kid" learns responsibility by repeated consequences. The more we can get him to do something, and something happens that he either likes or dislikes, the faster the behavior will change and an attitude will develop.

Big incentives or rewards that occur after a long period of time also do not work as well with the "behavior kid." At the beginning of the fall term, we may tell the teenager who has been slacking off his schoolwork, "If you have a B average by Christmas, we'll take you to Disney World for the holidays." Or, "If you do not get detention again for the rest of the term, we'll help you buy the mountain bike you want." If you offer this type of long-term incentive to some teenagers, they will work like crazy for three days after you spell out the expectation and consequence, but will rapidly slide back into the old behavior. Or they will not show any behavioural change until three days before the report card, and then they will study 24 hours a day. For this particular personality type, it might be better to use a short-term goal such as weekend privileges, based on a report of his performance in school for the week. If you decide to use a long-term goal, you could also get a weekly report from school and he could earn points toward that goal on a weekly basis. In other words, the teenager having difficulty in school would receive points each week for completing homework and class work, for paying attention in class, or for good behavior to avoid detention. If he has a certain amount of points at the end of the specified period, he can get his trip to Disney, his mountain bike, or another desired reward.

Avoid Giving Sentences

"Go to your room." "You're not allowed to watch television this weekend." "You can't use the phone for four weeks." "You will have to stay in after school for a week." These statements work well with some teenagers, but not with others. Some adolescents serve the sentence, then do the same thing again. Sentences are primarily given to change an attitude and to get a teenager to think differently. Sentences work with the "attitude kid," but not with some other personality types.

Some teenagers work better toward things when there are goals or incentives. If you do give these youngsters a sentence, you want to put a light at the end of the tunnel; that is, a way they can work toward something or get out of the sentence. For example, rather than say, "Because you have been doing poorly in school, you cannot use the phone for four weeks," it would be better to explain, "You are grounded from using the phone for four weeks because you are doing poorly in school. However, each evening that you do your homework and do not give me any trouble, you will be able to talk on the phone that night." For some teenagers, if all you give is a sentence, the only thing that you can be sure will happen is that they will not talk on the phone and will serve the sentence. Their attitude toward homework or schoolwork will probably not improve. However, if you give them a sentence with a light at the end of the tunnel (a way to work out of the sentence), you may get a better response regarding their homework and schoolwork.

Avoid Excessive Explaining, Lectures, and Reasoning

Teenagers look forward to lectures about as much as we do to a heart attack. Many parents talk, explain, reason, and lecture too much. For some adolescents, this approach will not benefit in developing a better understanding of the situation, nor will it help them to acquire responsible behaviours. Some teenagers will not accept explanations or reasons why they have to do something. One, five, fifty, or five hundred explanations will not satisfy them or make them understand. The only thing that will please them is what they want to hear. A teenager faced with a history test may ask, "Why do I have to study history? I'll never use it. It's dumb." After you offer numerous logical reasons and explanations of why history is an important subject, he is still objecting. The only thing that will satisfy him is for you to say, "Yes, you're right. History is dumb. Don't study for the test." However, you cannot respond in this fashion. Sometimes the only reason that it is necessary is "Because I said so."

Model Responsible Behaviours

We are very powerful models for our children. They learn both good and bad behaviours from watching us and seeing how we solve problems, deal with certain situations, or interact with people. If your teenager sees you acting in an irresponsible fashion or showing a lack of internal control, there is a strong probability that she will learn this type of behavior. Show her responsible actions.

Assign Chores

A large majority of parents feel that the performance of chores
or duties around the house is a big part of developing
responsibility. Giving teenager duties around the house will
not, by itself, develop responsibility, but it will help. When
assigning tasks, you must state not only what you expect, but
also what the consequences of failure to do the chores will be.
There are several ways to do this.

An allowance may be based on chores. A teenager gets a
certain amount of money for her allowance each week. Her
jobs are to clean the cat's litter box every day and wash the
dishes four times a week. Each time she does these chores
without being told, she earns a portion of her allowance. If she
does not do them without being told, she loses that portion of
her allowance. Whether she gets the full allowance at the end
of the week is totally her responsibility.

Another teenager's duty is to put his clothes away after they
are placed on his bed. The rule might state, "I won't wash any
more of your clothes until the clothes that have been placed
on your bed are put away."

The adolescent's duty is to feed the dog, but she never does it
without being told. Her mother might say, "You don't get your
supper until the dog is fed." The natural consequence of not
being responsible is that the teenager's supper is delayed and
she may get hungry.

A youngster may be told, "If the bathroom is clean by noon,
I'll drive you to your friend's house. If it is not clean by then,
I'll have to clean it. Since that will give me more work and
involve more of my time, I will not be able to drive you. You
will have to walk to your friend's."

The use of logical or natural consequences can centre around
chores. You tell a child, "This is *our* house and we are *all*
responsible for what has to be done in the house. Your father

has certain responsibilities, your sister has chores, I have many things to do to keep the house running, and you also have certain jobs. If you do not hold up your end and do not do what you are supposed to do, that means someone else will have to do it. When this happens, the other person has to use his or her time and energy to complete your responsibilities and will have less time and energy to do things for you." In other words, if the teenager cannot perform duties and tasks around the house to help other family members and make things easier for all involved, then the rest of the family will not do things for the teenager that will help him out or make things run more smoothly for him.

Chores can help develop self-discipline and responsibility, but they can also teach the adolescent to manipulate her parents if the parents do not consistently monitor the behavior. A teenager's chore is to clean her room before she leaves the house on Saturday. However, even though she does not always perform the task, she is still allowed to leave. If this happens, the parents are encouraging inappropriate behaviours and a lack of responsibility in the child.

In assigning chores, you must be very specific and define exactly what you mean by a clean room or a straightened kitchen. You must also specify the consequences of this behavior ahead of time. Your teenager's definition of a clean room may be different from yours, so it has to be clearly defined.

Once the rule and consequences are clearly spelled out, you should deal with a lack of compliance in a very calm and matter-of-fact way. For example, you tell your teenager, "You have to take out the trash by seven every night. If it is not taken out by then, I will take it out and you will not receive a portion of your allowance that day." If the chore is not completed, you should follow through with the specific consequence rather than nag, remind, lecture, or shout.

Distribute Chores Equally Among Siblings

If there are several children in the house, have them sit down and assign a weight or value to each chore. This will avoid arguments like, "I'm doing more work than my brother" or "My sister has an easier job than me." For example, the youngsters may decide that feeding the dog, emptying the dishwasher, and similar activities have a value of 1 point. Cleaning the table after meals, sweeping the kitchen, and similar activities are worth 2 points. Vacuuming, putting away clothes, and other jobs may have a value of 3 points. Cleaning the bathroom may be worth 4 points. By assigning different weights or values to activities, the children can feel that the system is fair and they are not doing more work than their siblings. If a child cleans the bathroom, which has a value of 4 points, another child may have to do four activities valued at 1 point each that day to equal his sister's work. Another way to create a fair situation among siblings when it comes to chores is to vary the activities. On a calendar you could write the child's name on the day he is supposed to do a particular chore. For example, if you have two children, Jason and Alan, and one of their chores is to feed the dog, you could alternate the initial J or A on the calendar every other day. When it came time to feed the dog, all you would have to do is look at the calendar to see whose day it is. By using this method, one child would not feel as if he has fed the dog ten times for every one time his brother completed the chore.

When, as a family, you establish the methods you'll use to share chores, set up at the start a time, place, and agenda for discussing how all of this is working.

Give an Allowance

An allowance is a fixed amount of money given to children on a periodic basis (weekly, biweekly, monthly). They could receive the allowance for doing nothing other than breathing or they could earn the allowance for performing household chores or duties. If an allowance system is put into practice in your home, base it on some type of work or behavior. It need not be a significant amount of work, but receiving the allowance should be contingent upon some type of behavior or job. An allowance system can often be used to help children develop responsibility or to teach them the value of money. However, there are several things that must be kept in mind when implementing such a system.

The range of incentives and rewards greatly decreases as children get older. For the adolescent, the range is somewhat small and often directly or indirectly involves money. When deciding whether an allowance should be used for a particular chore or be contingent on a certain level of cooperation or behavior, the first question that must be asked is how important money is to the child. Some professionals feel that children should not receive money for certain behaviours, while others think it is all right. Some people feel that children should not be paid for things they are supposed to do. Money can be used as a reward or an incentive, but an allowance system is appropriate only if the teenager values or needs money. Some parents say they have instituted an allowance system, but it does not work. In many cases, the reason for this is that the teenager does not care about money, and to him one dollar is the same as one thousand dollars.

Another factor in deciding whether an allowance system should be implemented is "Does the teenager need money?" You tell a child that he will receive an allowance of £5.00 a week for putting out the bins and walking the dog. He does not complete the chores and does not get the allowance.

However, any time he is with you at the store and wants a soda, you buy it for him. At the shopping mall when he feels like playing a video game, you give him money to play. On Saturday you pay for him to go to a movie. Why does this child need his own money? He doesn't, because he is getting everything he wants. Whether he does the chores or not, he is still able to get the money he needs to fulfil his wants. A parent instituted an allowance system for her twelve-year-old daughter for performing chores around the home. The first week the allowance system worked beautifully, but after that it did not work. When the young girl was asked why she was not doing the chores, she said that any time she needed money she could go next door to her grandparents and they would give her all the money she needed. If an allowance system is used, you must dry up other sources of income in order to produce a need for money.

Another way to make the allowance system work is to specify certain activities or items that you will not pay for or purchase for the teenager. In other words, you tell the child that he will be given a certain allowance each week for doing certain duties. He is to use this money for going out on the weekend, buying gas for the car, playing video games, or anything else he wants. You will not pay for any of these material things or activities. If they are important items to the child, he will then need the allowance to pay for them himself.

The amount of allowance a child receives is based on two general factors: your financial situation and the needs of the teenager. However, it should be kept in mind that you can give too much allowance. This may create a situation where the teenager accumulates money. When he has enough, he does not have to work because the need for money does not exist. The purpose of the allowance system is thus defeated. You must assess the needs of the teenager and try to base the allowance accordingly. Naturally, a younger adolescent does not need as much spending money as an older one. What you expect a child to do with this money should be realistic. For example, it may be very difficult for a fifteen-year-old who receives ten dollars a week to use this allowance for both his lunch at school and movies on the weekend. Find out how much things cost today and try to become aware of your teenager's needs and the cost for him to fulfil these needs. Be sure you and your child have the same idea of what is expected and what the consequences will be.

If the teenager does not earn the allowance, he should not receive it. If he earns the allowance, you must be certain that he receives it. You must be consistent. If you are inconsistent with payment of the allowance, the teenager may manipulate you or not complete the task, or his motivation may decrease and his performance may be affected. If he performs the chores assigned, he should receive his allowance on a regular basis. In addition, you should never take away all or part of his allowance when the adolescent has earned it by completing his specific assignments. This will also decrease the effectiveness of the system. For example, a teenager has earned all of his allowance for helping around the house with various chores. On Friday when he is to receive his allowance, he comes home with a detention and because of the detention he is not given the total allowance. As a result, the next week when it comes to motivating him to do chores, he is probably not going to comply.

An allowance earned should be received. But be consistent and do not give the child the allowance if he has not earned it.

All teenagers occasionally grow angry and rebellious and express these emotions in some fashion. Some methods of acknowledging aggressive feelings produce problems, others don't.

Anger and feelings of disapproval build up and then are released through different methods. We can exemplify this situation by using the image of an "anger" balloon. Each time something happens that we do not like, air is forced into the balloon and it starts to expand. Eventually, air has to be let out of the balloon. How anger is expressed is different for different people. Some people let anger build up until their balloon pops, and when this happens there may be an explosive outburst of anger over a minor annoyance. After this display of anger, there is usually a period of control until the balloon blows up again. Other people release air from the balloon every time it starts to fill. These are the individuals who appropriately express their feelings at the time they occur. Some other individuals release air through passive-aggressive manoeuvres, displacement, or physical complaints. In addition to helping the teenager appropriately express and deal with his or her angry feelings, parents should try to reduce the accumulation of anger and deal appropriately with aggressive and rebellious behaviours when they occur. The techniques that follow should help.

Encourage Appropriate Communication

The most effective way to deal with anger and rebellious behavior is to have teenagers appropriately communicate their feelings of disapproval and resentment. Encourage them to express and explain negative feelings, sources of anger, and their opinions—that is, what angers them, what we do that they do not like, what they disapprove of. If a teenager expresses emotions appropriately, in a normal tone of voice, she should not be viewed as rude or disrespectful. This is an appropriate expression of anger, and the youngster should not be reprimanded or punished. In other words, allow teenagers to complain, disagree, or disapprove, provided they are not sarcastic, flippant, or nasty. Remember, though, that allowing a child to shout, swear, or be fresh does not teach effective communication of emotions.

Listen. If the teenager is complaining about excessive restrictions, punishments, or other things that she does not like, *listen.* Try to understand her feelings. If the complaints are realistic, see if something can be worked out and resolved, or if a compromise can be achieved.

Avoid Excessive Negative Attention

It's a mistake to pay more attention to what the child is doing wrong—his failures, mistakes, misbehaviours—than to what he is doing right—his successes, achievements, good behaviours. When you go to bed at night, review the day you have had with your child. Have you spent as much time during the day looking at his appropriate behaviours as you have looking at his inappropriate actions? You should avoid using punishment as a primary method of control. Instead, substitute positive consequences, which place the emphasis on good behavior rather than on bad behavior. Eliminate verbal punishment (hollering, putting down the adolescent, name-calling, excessive criticism), and use reward as a disciplinary tactic. Emphasize successes, accomplishments, achievements, and good behaviours. Pay more attention to normal good behavior and be positive.

Constant nagging of a teenager will certainly result in a build-up of anger, resentment, and aggressive behaviours.

Try Not to React to Passive-Aggressive Behavior

Some of the opposition, stubbornness, resistance, and other passive-aggressive manoeuvres of teenagers are designed to express anger and/or to get a reaction from the parents. Ignoring this behavior is often an effective way to reduce it. Some ways of dealing with this passive-aggressive behavior will result in the development of more anger, while others will help deflate the anger balloon. For example, a child is told to set the table for dinner. While setting the table, she mumbles under her breath and every now and then you hear comments like, "They think I'm a slave. I want to go live at Grandma's, where I'm appreciated." Along with the mumbling, she is angrily tossing ice in the glasses and banging down the plates and silverware. This teenager is annoyed because she feels she has better things to do than set the table. Her mumbling and other actions are passive-aggressive manoeuvres to express her anger and resentment. These behaviours are releasing anger and letting air out of the anger balloon. If you react to her mumbling by criticizing or scolding, you will be putting more air back into the balloon—that is, the anger that was initially released by the child's complaining and defiance will be offset by a build-up of additional aggressive feelings. By using the consequence of ignoring her, this additional build-up of anger can be eliminated.

There are several things that must be kept in mind when using this consequence, and there are a few different ways to ignore the behavior. In general, if you ask a teenager to do something and he is doing it, although complaining the whole time, ignore his complaints since he is doing what you asked.

Avoid Random Discipline

Parents often discipline after the fact. I call this random discipline. They set a rule and wait for the adolescent to break it before they decide upon a consequence. To teenagers, the concept of fairness is extremely important. If they are disciplined in this fashion, they may frequently feel unjustly treated. In addition, random discipline often makes teenagers feel that others are responsible for what has happened to them and anger is apt to develop. You should spell out the rules and consequences for your child's behavior at the same time. The most important part of this process is not the rule, but the consequence. Put the responsibility for what happens to the child squarely on his or her shoulders.

Don't Get into a Power Struggle

You tell the adolescent to clean his room and he refuses. Then you threaten, "You had better clean it, or you're not going out on Saturday." He replies, "You can't make me clean it and I'm going out on Saturday, anyway." Then you say something, he says something, you both begin to shout, and a full-blown power struggle has developed. This is a good way to generate anger in your child.

When possible, avoid battles and power struggles, which only lead to a build-up of anger. At times, it may be better to have the child experience the consequence of his behavior rather than to win the battle and get him to do what you want. If you try to win each fight, you may battle the child throughout adolescence, and will probably end up losing the war.

Look for Ways to Compromise

In many situations with adolescents, you should try to treat them the way you would one of your friends or another adult. Rather than get into a battle to see who is going to win, it may be better to create a situation where a compromise is reached.

Provide Appropriate Models

Children learn a great deal from modelling their parents' behavior. The way we handle our conflicts and problems is apt to be imitated by our children. If I handle my anger by hollering, throwing things, or hitting, there is a good possibility that my children will handle their conflicts in a similar fashion. The old saying "Don't do as I do; do as I say" is a very ineffective way of dealing with behavior. Therefore, if you see aggressive or rebellious behaviours in your teenager, look at yourself, your spouse, or an older sibling to see if one of you is modelling these behaviours. If so, the behavior must stop before we can expect to change the adolescent's conduct.

If there is a significant amount of arguing in the home, or if parents demonstrate disrespect for one another, it is likely that the teenager will adopt similar behavior patterns. If you scream at your child, he is likely to scream back.

One mother told me, "Every time I hit my daughter, she hits me back. What should I do?" My answer was very simple: "Stop hitting her." Whenever I see a child who is showing aggressive-type behaviours, I want to know if this behavior is being modelled in the home. If youngsters are dealt with through physical punishment, we may be teaching them to handle conflicts by physical force or aggressive behavior. It does not have to be the actual use of physical force. It can be threats of force. In other words, "I'm going to get you to do that because I am bigger than you and can control you by intimidation." If we deal with teenagers in that fashion, we are apt to cause a build-up of anger at the same time that we are indirectly teaching them aggressive and inappropriate methods of problem solving.

Parents who use physical punishment with the young child, as a primary method of dealing with his or her behavior, forget one important thing: children grow and usually get as big as or bigger than them. A young child disciplined through physical punishment will probably end up as an adolescent who gets into physical battles with his parents.

Parents must look at themselves to be sure they are not models of the behavior they are trying to eliminate in the child. Serving as an appropriate model is a good way to teach children how to deal with and express anger.

Who's in Control?

When I was a young parent, people would tell me, "Little kids, little problems. Big kids, big problems." At the time, I did not quite understand this bit of advice, but now that I have experienced being the parent of teenagers, I know exactly what it means.

Young children who have been pampered and spoiled—and have learned how to control their parents—are used to having things their own way. Therefore, they tend to be somewhat bossy and self-cantered behaviours that intensify during adolescence. If a child like this is told not to eat any cookies, he may defy the parents, sneak into the kitchen, and eat the cookies. Or if he is told not to jump on the couch, he does not listen and continues jumping. When adolescence arrives, the same child is told to be home by midnight and instead comes home at 4:00 A.M. Told not to drink and drive, he drinks and drives anyway. The little problems of the small child become much bigger during adolescence, and frequently result in more serious consequences.

I often see families where adolescents are out of control, will not take no for an answer, and will not accept parental authority. Many times when these teens do not get their way, aggressive, rebellious, and oppositional behaviour results. Some of these adolescents have been in control of the family since they were young. The child determined the routines and activities in the home more than the parents. A seven-year-old was having trouble in school because she was not doing the required work in class, but instead was daydreaming and doing whatever she pleased. In talking with the parents, I discovered that they were having the same type of difficulty at home. The child would not cooperate, especially with routine tasks. They also mentioned that she was constantly complaining to them about the fact that her three- and four-year-old brothers did not have to go to school. Why did she have to? She did not think it was fair that her brothers could stay home, play, and watch television. Every morning before school, an argument about this usually took place. She frequently requested to stay home, and generally this issue produced a great deal of conflict in the home. In order to solve the situation, the parents put the two brothers in nursery school, demonstrating that the daughter was more in control than the parents. Rather than allow a child to call the shots and try to manipulate the environment to accommodate the child or to avoid problems, it might be better to have the child learn that there are certain things that must be done whether or not she wants to do them.

As I mentioned earlier, we can control young children, but with the adolescent we must exert authority. I am not talking about an authority by force or by dictatorship. I am talking about an authority that involves setting rules and being consistent in administering consequences. If parents can exert this type of authority, the probability that positive behaviours and attitudes can be developed will increase.

The child who has been in control his entire life finds it difficult to relinquish this power during adolescence. However, because of the severity of the consequences that can occur in adolescence, parents are usually trying to exert more control at this time. As a result, battles, conflicts, anger, and resentment occur when the teenager does not have his own way. Below are some techniques on establishing rules and consequences in a fashion that will allow you to have some authority over the teenager.

Stabilise the Environment

Teenagers who experience environmental change—especially divorce, separation, or remarriage—may develop underlying anger. The anger and resentment that result from the changes may be expressed in other ways. Try to identify the changes, stabilize the environment, and get him to express his feelings through more appropriate methods. If the adolescent has questions regarding a divorce or remarriage, discuss them with him.

Avoid Excessive Restrictions

Some children who are overprotected, excessively restricted, and generally not allowed to be like other youngsters their age may develop resentment and anger. They want to do things that others do, but are prevented from doing so. Sometimes you have to look at your teenager's peer group in order to decide what is and is not appropriate, and what is too much restriction.

Do Not Let the Behavior Get Out of Control

Once a child is actively involved in an aggressive behaviour or shouting match, it is difficult to deal with the behavior. Rather than wait till the behavior occurs to handle it, sometimes it is possible, and better, to try to prevent it from happening or to catch it early and not let it get out of control. In some teenagers, the aggressive behaviour develops gradually and may involve several steps. Some initial behaviour appears and then intensifies. For example, a teenager's brother may call him stupid. Some verbal exchanges follow, then a pushing and shoving match begins, and finally a full-blown fight erupts. Rather than wait to react when the fight starts, it would be better to try to catch the behavior early, and intervene before the situation gets out of hand. Target the name-calling or verbal arguing and try to stop that, rather than wait to zero in on the fighting.

A mother tells her sixteen-year-old son to clean his room. When he says no, she counters back with a warning, then a threat. A struggle develops, and after some shouting and screaming on both parts, the boy goes to his room and throws something, breaking the window. Rather than waiting to zero in on the boy's destructive behavior, it would be better for the parent to catch this kind of sequence in the beginning.

Chapter 22

Dealing with Daily Teen Behaviours

Parents express many specific concerns about their adolescent's attitudes and behaviours. However, before addressing some of the specific topics in later sections, here is some general information on effective techniques of behavior management that should help you deal with your child on a daily basis. How do you get the child to cooperate more around the house? What can you do to get him to clean his room or to have him come in on time? How do you improve her flippant attitude or get her to stop aggravating her sister? Some of the techniques presented here are guaranteed to make your day run smoother and reduce some conflict in your home. I suggest you read this section before proceeding with the rest of the book, because many of the sections that follow are based on the techniques presented here.

In general, you will first want to analyze the behavior you are trying to deal with. Then spell out the rule or expectation *and* the consequence at the same time, *before* the rule is broken. Say what you mean and mean what you say. Follow through with what you say and be consistent.

Analyse the Behaviour

In discussing the adolescent's behavior, many parents remark: "He does not want to be part of the family," "My daughter is depressed and unhappy," "She's not motivated in school," "His problem is he's always angry," "My son is constantly irritating everybody," "She is immature." My first response is to ask the parent, "Can you give me an example of what you mean when you say he does not want to be part of the family?" "What behavior is the child showing that makes you think he is angry?" "What is he doing to irritate everybody?" "What is your child doing that makes you think she is immature?" In other words, I ask the parents to look at the behavior in more specific terms rather than in general terms. What I mean when I say, "My daughter is depressed," might be that she has lost interest in things that were important to her. What you mean when you say, "My daughter is depressed," might be that she stays in her room all the time and cries easily. Lack of motivation in school could mean a variety of things: the child is capable of A's and B's, but is getting only C's; she is not studying for tests; she does not complete homework; or she daydreams in class.

Be Specific

Before any behaviour can be dealt with or changed, it first must be specified or stated in detail. Although it might not be possible to make your son become more a "part of the family," you may be able to get him to spend more time out of his room and become more involved in family interaction. If you say your teen is angry, what exactly is he doing? Is he continually muttering under his breath, making faces when you try to tell him something, slamming doors, or generally getting very upset and volatile over minor difficulties? What is the immaturity you worry about in your daughter? Is she fifteen years old and still needing your help in getting dressed for school?

Many parents find it somewhat difficult to look at specific behaviours', because it is normal to talk about our children in very general terms. However, the first step in changing any behavior is to be specific. Try to avoid vague, general terms, and identify the exact behavior or behaviours that are of concern and what you would like to change.

Look at the Behavior Sequence

Once the behaviour has been described in detail, you can then analyze the entire behavior sequence. For example, let's take the child who will never take no for an answer. How did he get this way?

Parent: My child will never accept no for an answer.

Psychologist: What do you mean by that? Can you give me an example?

Parent: I just can't tell him no. If everything is going his way and he is getting to do whatever he wants and is not told no, everything is fine. However, when we tell him he cannot do what he wants, he gets upset and argues and cannot accept what we have told him. He used our car all last week; then last night when he asked to use the car again, we refused and he became very upset and started arguing.

Psychologist: What did he say to you?

Parent: He was really shouting and told us how mean we were and how all his friends' parents let them use the car whenever they wanted to. He also mentioned that we used to let his brother have the car whenever he wanted and that we were putting too many restrictions on him. We were not being fair and did not understand his situation.

Psychologist: What did you do?

Parent: We told him that we need to use the car and that he just could not have it whenever he wanted. A car is expensive to operate and he would have to try to use it less often and get rides with his friends. He can have it to go specific places, not just to joyride all around the city. After many attempts to try to reason calmly with him and explain why we said no, my husband and I became upset with his attitude and unwillingness to see our position.

Psychologist: What happened next?

Parent: Because he had an answer for everything we told him, pretty soon we started arguing back at him. After a while, we became totally exasperated and tired of the verbal battle, so we gave him the keys to the car and told him to leave in order for us all to calm down.

In the above example, if the child listened to his parents he would not use the car. However, by aggravating, not taking "no" for an answer, he was able to use the car. The reason this behavior occurs - and continues - is because it works!

Let's take another example, the child who does not cooperate without an argument or fuss, and who always has something to say if you ask her to do something.

Parent: Every time I ask my child to do something, she complains, "I'm not a slave. Why do I have to do this? My brother doesn't have to. You're always making me do things." She has just a few jobs to do around the house, but each time we ask her, she'll either put off the chore and not do it, or give us a hard time.

Psychologist: Give me an example of what you mean.

Parent: The other night I asked her to put out the garbage. She started mumbling and complaining and making faces, then grabbed the garbage can and dragged it out to the curb, banging it every inch of the way. You would think I had asked her to paint the house or lay the lawn.

Psychologist: But she did put out the bin?

Parent: Yes, but the whole time she was complaining and acting as if she did not want to do what she was asked.

Psychologist: What did you do next?

Parent: I tried to ignore most of what she said but she was starting to irritate me, so I began explaining everything that her father and I did for her. I asked how she would like it if every time she asked us to do something we made a scene or complained. I told her that she had only a few chores to do and that I did not feel as if it were a burden for her to do a few simple things for me when I did so much for her. She continued mumbling and I continued yelling, and she eventually stalked off to her room.

In situations like the above, what I have asked the parents to do is to analyze the behaviour. They should not only look at the *behaviour* - the unwillingness to take no for an answer (example 1) or the mumbling and complaining (example 2) - but also look at what comes before the behavior (*antecedents*) and what comes after it (the *consequence*). In any behaviour sequence there are three parts:

ANTECEDENTS, BEHAVIOR, AND CONSEQUENCE: A→B→C

A	B	C
Antecedents	**Behavior**	**Consequence**
Asks to use the car. Told, "No."	Will not accept. Argues.	Gets to use the car.
Told to do a chore	Mumbles. Complains.	Parent gets upset.

In looking at the entire behaviour sequence, we have taken the first step in dealing with the behaviour. We have not only looked at the specific behaviour, but have also seen what comes before the action and what comes after it. We have to look at the entire sequence before attempting to change it.

In analyzing behaviour, it is also important to see how often it occurs - that is, how many times a day, hour, or week. Does it occur ten times a day, once a week, or three times an hour? There are a couple of reasons for looking at how frequently behaviour occurs. I have had many parents tell me, "Once I started looking at the behaviour closely and keeping a record of how frequently it occurred, I realized that it was not as bad as I thought it was. I thought he and his brother were fighting continuously but the fights only occurred a couple of times a day." Another reason for looking at frequency of behaviour is that the child usually does not wake up one morning behaving a certain way. The behaviour develops gradually over a period of weeks, months, or years. Therefore, in changing the behaviour, a similar process will occur. A gradual improvement over time will take place.

Usually, when parents look at the child's actions in general terms (e.g., anger, immaturity, uncooperativeness), they cannot see the small changes that occur. For example, parents may tell me, "Our child never talks to us. He never communicates anything, and we don't know what is going on in his life." I might then try some interventions and give the parents suggestions to improve the communication. After a few weeks, if the parents looked only at the overall behaviour, they might still feel the child was uncommunicative and not as talkative as he used to be when he was younger. However, if they had observed the child's behaviour more closely in order to see how frequently he was communicating, they might have seen an improvement. They might have realized that before the treatment plan was started, the child spoke to them only a couple of times or only when he needed something. However, after a few weeks of trying some interventions, the child was now communicating five to seven times a day and was volunteering information about school, friends, and activities. Looking at the overall behaviour and comparing it to when the child was younger, it may still seem as if he is not talking very much. However, if we look at the frequency of the behaviour, knowing that behaviour changes gradually, we can see a considerable improvement from when the treatment plan was started. We have to look for small improvements and movements toward a goal, and not for a dramatic change overnight.

In analyzing behaviour in this way, we look at the important factors in behaviour change - the consequences. The reason most of us do what we do is that we know the consequences of our behaviour. If the consequences of behaviour were always the same, and, for example, you were paid whether you went to work or stayed home, you would be foolish to go to work. The same holds true for adolescents. The teenagers in the two examples behaved the way they did because they already knew the consequences of their behaviour. They got what they wanted.

The following may be somewhat similar to what goes on unconsciously, or sometimes consciously, with your child.

Psychologist: Your mother tells me that you never do anything the first time you are told. She has to tell you over and over again, and get upset and yell, before you do anything, such as cleaning your room.

Adolescent: My mother is always talking and telling me to do stuff. She gives me a hundred lectures a day and asks me to do a lot of stupid things, like cleaning my room. I usually put off doing what she says because the first thirty times she tells me, she uses a normal tone of voice and is pretty calm, so I don't think she really means it.

Psychologist: Then what happens?

Adolescent: Around the thirty-first time, her voice starts getting a little bit louder. She's getting upset now, and around the thirty-second or thirty-third time, she starts hollering and saying in a very angry voice, "I really mean it. You'd better clean your room!" Somewhere around the thirty-fourth and thirty-fifth time she says it, the vein in her neck starts sticking out, her face turns red, and she's really screaming now.

Psychologist: What do you do then?

Adolescent: Well, finally I know she means business, because the hair on the back of her neck is standing up. So I go clean the room or do whatever else she wants me to do.

Psychologist: It sounds as if you wait for the right signal or cue that tells you a consequence is coming or something is really going to happen. When you know she means business, that's when you do what your mother requests.

Adolescent: That's right.

There are many other examples that could be used, but the point is that people often behave as they do because of the consequences of their behavior - what they get out of it or what happens to them as a result of it. Much behaviour in the adolescent are present because of the consequences. Whenever people relate to or interact with one another, parents and adolescents included, they teach each other certain behaviours based primarily on consequences. When we interact with our children, we are teaching them behaviours and they are teaching us to respond to them in certain ways. We may teach children how to be dependent, fresh, or immature, or how not to take no for an answer, not to listen, or the like. At the same time, they may teach us how to scold, nag, scream, get upset, criticize, or worry. It stands to reason that if we can teach children certain unacceptable behaviours; we can also teach them acceptable behaviours. This is true, but most of us go about it the wrong way, by focusing directly on the children and trying to change them. It is very difficult to change another's behavior without changing our own. It is much easier if parents change the way they relate to their teenagers, and, as a result, the youngsters change their behavior and the way they relate to the parents. I am *not* implying, as some mental health professionals do, that parents are the cause of *all* behavior difficulties in children. Children can cause problems in a family as well as parents can cause problems in children. However, it is easier for adults to change their behavior than to try directly to change the teenager's behavior.

Much of the behavior seen in people is the result of consequences and a person's response to environmental conditions. Often, without a change in environment, it will be difficult to change the behavior. If the surroundings and reactions of others are modified, however, it will be easier to alter it. While it is much easier to modify a young child's environment than an adolescent, your behavior and your response to the child are part of the environment and can be changed. By responding to children differently, you can change the influence of their behavior. Just as important as analyzing the child's behavior, parents need to look closely at what they themselves are doing and how they are responding to situations. If parents can change both their reactions and the types of consequences used to deal with the teenager, they in turn may modify their teenager's behavior.

Giving Orders a Teen Can Understand

Your teen is far more concerned about her complexion than she is about the state of your household, and you can save both time and angst by clearly communicating what is bothering you. Be specific. Just as a toddler responds better to "pick up the blocks" than to "clean up your room," the same is true for a teen.

You can make your expectations even more clearly by creating a checklist. For example, an index card taped to the mirror in the bathroom might bear this post-shower checklist:
Wring out washcloth and hang on side of tub.
Hang towels on bar.
Use bathmat to dry up puddles on floor and hang over edge of tub.
Put shampoo back in cupboard

For a while, you may have to remind your child of her new responsibilities—expect to, and don't get angry. You're teaching a new behavior, one that she has been able to avoid doing for a good number of years.

If your child still doesn't comply after a time, though, you'll need to take stronger action. Establish age appropriate consequence.

Its best if the consequence has something to do with the offense: "If you don't have time to help around the house, then that means I have to devote extra time. For that reason, I won't be able to drive you to the game this weekend."

If a new habit has been particularly difficult to develop, you might consider reward system. For example, if he remembers to clean up after himself in the kitchen for a full month (with two days off for bad days), its worth a new CD. After a month of good behavior, chances are good that the reform will be complete. (Remember, though, that this is a reward system, not a payment. After earning the first reward, your child should be expected to do the jobs on his own.)

As each new behavior becomes habit (when you're no longer tripping over his size 11 sneakers as you come in the door, because he's finally "gotten the message"), add a new one or two without making a big issue of it.

In an ideal world, no one else would have to empty someone else's pockets before throwing jeans in the wash, remove clothing from the floor, or trip over backpacks and shoes left all over the house. Though nirvana is difficult to reach, you should set "improvement" as a goal. Choose the responsibilities you want your teen to handle, and with love and patience keep reminding her of them.

Throughout their school years, teenagers are subject to a lot of stress. There's more to learn than ever before, and a much greater emphasis on grades, especially at GCSE and A level.

It's no wonder that they feel under constant pressure to learn, achieve and perform.

While much of the stress comes from school situations, especially at exam time, social factors – friends, boyfriends, girlfriends – can also contribute to the feelings.

Stress Symptoms

There are many ways in which stress can manifest itself, both physical and mental, and you need to be aware of them all, and alert to the signs. Stress is a major problem among teens, possibly even more than it is among adults, because they don't have the experience or maturity to be able to cope with it.

Physically, at times it can be hard to distinguish stress from a normal teenage rebellion. There could be moodiness or defiance, but it would seem more extreme than usual. If your teen is depressed or appears sad for extended periods, this, too, could indicate stress. Sometimes the physical signs are quite apparent, with the onset of asthma attacks or eczema on the skin, in which case you should take your teen to the doctor immediately. Stomach aches and headaches occur commonly when someone is stressed. You can treat the immediate symptoms at home usually, but you still need to address the underlying cause.

Swings in appetite could be a sign, whether it's eating far more or far less than normal, whilst problems sleeping, especially if accompanied by nightmares, stand as a definite indicator. If your teen begins smoking, or using drugs, it could be due to stress, too, as could not being able to concentrate properly on schoolwork.

Perhaps the hardest thing to deal with is if you teen begins experiencing panic attacks. These can be terrifying, not only to the victim, but to those around. Again, you can get them over the attack, but you still need to help them deal with the stress in order to stop them completely.

What You Can Do

The biggest thing you can do is not put any pressure on them yourself, asking why they're not achieving better marks, for instance. Think about it: it's bad enough for them at school without you adding to the demands. Make sure they have plenty of free time, rather than a packed schedule of activities – teens need to relax too!

Watch them and talk to them. If they seem to be suffering from stress, gently point out that they seem to be upset, angry, or whatever. Certainly never tell them to get on and snap out of it. You need to empathise, not criticise!

Be on their side, and see their point of view. Be sympathetic in your comments and put yourself in their position. If there are specific, concrete problems to overcome, work on a solution with them. It builds a bond between you, and that can be useful with the next problem that occurs.

You have to be willing to initiate the conversation about stress. All too often teens don't have the experience to understand what's happening, but you do. You might suggest going for a walk together, and talking as you go. Different surroundings can encourage conversation, and exercise can also be beneficial, especially if done regularly, as stress relief. Break big problems down into smaller, more manageable ones and work on the answers to them with your teen. It helps them gain confidence, and can certainly reduce stress levels once they learn these things aren't insurmountable.

Be available to give emotional support, especially at exam times, when the stress is at its greatest. Make the time to talk, and encourage them to discuss their worries and fears. Simply talking about them can lessen them. You can't solve all their problems, and nor should you – part of growing up is learning to deal with them. But you can help them along the path.

It's very common for teens to say they want to leave school as soon as possible - in other words, at the end of the school year when they turn 16. However, saying it and meaning it can be two completely different things. How do you decide which is real, and when your teen truly wants to leave, what do you do?

opportunities for advancement. Often employers will even help pay for further education. You might not see it as an entirely satisfactory outcome, but at 18 they're adults, and you have to trust them to ultimately make their own decisions, be they right or wrong. Also, after working for a while, there's nothing to stop them applying to university - that's worth remembering.

When is it Real?

After being at school from the age of five, or possibly even younger, by the time they turn 16 and are facing GCSE exams it's natural for even academic teens to feel as if they've had enough of education. They might be earning money from a Saturday job and have friends who are a bit older and working and the lure of money in their pockets and freedom from homework can seem very attractive.

But when they do go on about leaving, do they mean it? Those who can obviously do well in A levels and with a university career ahead generally don't. It's a simple act of rebellion. For others, leaving seems the perfectly natural option. You need to sit down and talk to them to discover how deep the emotions run within them, as well as deciding what you're going to say. In some cases encouraging them to leave can be the best thing. In others, gentle persuasion to stay on is the right tactic.

Those Who Should Stay
Point out the advantages in staying where it seems reasonable, and how they'll end up doing something they'll enjoy as a job (don't emphasise that fact that it means two more years at school and another three or more at university!), with a greater choice, and the greater income they'll make in the long run. Point out that sixth-form colleges offer another, freer option. The more attractive you make it, the more likely they'll be to stay on.

We all naturally want our children to have better lives than we've had. But saying "You're staying on, and that's that!" is never a good move. Laying down the law might seem like the right thing, but with a volatile teen, all you'll often find is that they'll dig in their heels, and compromise becomes harder. Softly, softly should be the watchwords. Win them over gently and slowly instead. You know that in the end they'll thank you, but they can't see that yet.

Leaving after GCSEs
For those who are less academically inclined, leaving school really is a good option. But that shouldn't necessarily mean jumping directly into a job. The simple truth is that with limited qualifications they're going to be stuck in low-paid jobs that offer very little future. For those teens, college offers an ideal option. In many cases they can combine it with work, study something that interests them - the range of courses available can be quite staggering - and come out with both work experience and a qualification to prepare them for the future. In today's world, those pieces of paper count for a lot, and by not encouraging your teen to go to college, you're doing them a disservice.
Apprenticeships are nowhere near as common today as they once were, but for some it does offer an alternative route,

especially in the trades. They learn, and once again gain a qualification. For those who are inclined towards these kinds of jobs, they can make a huge long-term difference once they're journeymen.

Leaving After A Levels

University isn't the free proposition it once was, and the cost of a degree education can be a burden, either to parents or to students taking out loans. It will certainly discourage some, and there are many others who simply don't want to go on to university.

If you believe they could manage a degree, encourage it, and offer as much support and encouragement as possible. But with several A levels under their belts, teens can at least generally find jobs that pay a little more.

Bullying

Bullying is an endemic problem, mostly in schools, but you'll even find it in the workplace, too. Many children, teens and younger, are bullied every year, and although schools and education authorities are doing plenty to stop it, it can seem like a losing battle, especially if your child is a victim.

It can be difficult to know if your teen is being bullied; after all, it's something they don't want to talk about, and certainly not admit to their parents. They often feel they have to deal with it themselves. But bullying can seriously affect lives – there are teens who've killed themselves because of prolonged, excessive bullying.

Bullying doesn't have to be physical. In some ways the mental and emotional bullying is worse, and certainly more insidious. But the first thing you have to do is find out whether your teen is being bullied.

The Signs

You might not notice the signs at first, but they do build up. If your teen seems to lose possessions regularly, it's often not carelessness, but they're being taken, and the same with any money they might have.

Are they quieter, and seem withdrawn and depressed? Do they come straight home from school and don't go out at night the way they used to? Are they moodier than usual, and have they become more isolated, falling out with good friends and having trouble sleeping? Then there's a good chance that they're the victims of bullying.

Of course, there are the more obvious physical signs, such as bruises, scrapes, lacerations and torn clothing. If you see those, you know there's something going on.

What to Do

Talk gently and casually to your team. Don't ask if they're being bullied, but inquire about the general situation at school, and work your way around to ask if anything is worrying them, as they seem tense and stressed. Make sure they know you're concerned about their health.

They might deny being bullied, but if you take the soft approach and use patience, in the end you'll probably hear the truth, even if they won't name the bullies.

When you discover what's happening, don't rant and rage. Stay calm and tell your teen that you'll work on the problem with them.

One thing you do need to do is inform the school, Make an appointment with the head teacher as lay out all you know for him. He will probably want your teen to attend the meeting, but if fear is a big factor, you can say no to that. Tell him that you expect him to investigate and act on the problem immediately, and don't take no for an answer. If there's been a physical assault, you should also involve the police (although your teen might ask you not to).

Internet and Mobile Phone Bullying

Online bullying, through instant messages, e-mails and posting on bulletin boards have risen hugely in the last few years, as have threatening mobile phone text messages. Usually these are anonymous, which can pose a problem, but you can fight them.

With e-mails, you can easily discover the service provider of the sender, and contact them (usually abuse@whatevertheisp.co.uk). They can then identify and block the sender. With instant messages, if they're insistent and threatening, print them and inform the police, as well as blocking the sender. With bulletin boards, there, contact the host and inform them, and demand politely that they take action.

With mobile phones, it can be trickier. Again, if there's an ongoing pattern, record when the texts were received and what they said, and inform the police, because these comprise harassment. Even when the number is masked, it's possible to identify the caller. You can also get a new SIM card with a different number for your teen – but you need to make sure that number is only given to friends.

You really can help your teen if he or she is being bullied, but a lot depends on you remaining actively involved in their lives, and making sure there's a bond where they feel they can talk to you and open up properly. Bullying can be beaten. It's not easy, it takes time, effort, and guts, especially on the part of your teen, but it can be done.

Chapter 23

How to Live with Your Adult Teen

They're called Generation Y--the growing numbers of young adults who promptly move back home after college, or perhaps never move out at all, in an effort to save money while searching for a perfect job. Living with your grown child can be a stressful tug of war for control: Your child makes his own decisions, but you still rule the roost. Read on to find some tips and suggestions to make living with your adult child a little easier on everyone in your household.

Have a serious talk with your child about the situation. Make sure you both agree to the terms and conditions of the arrangement. Living together will take compromises on both parts, and it will be easier if you keep lines of communication open and set expectations beforehand.
As a parent, you'll have to accept that your child is an adult and can make his own decisions, and your child will have to realize that living in your house might entail more rules than he is used to.

Although your child is an adult, he is still living in your house, and therefore should be expected to respect boundaries. Establish house rules before your child returns home, and make sure to enforce them. On the other hand, your child is an adult, and his boundaries of privacy should also be respected. House rules could be related to having house guests or parties, and your stance on smoking and drinking alcohol. Just remember, although your child should be expected to abide by the rules of your house, they should be age-appropriate. For example, setting a curfew for your child might not be realistic, but expecting him to call if he isn't coming home for the night is.

Rent, groceries, utility bills--all of these are a factor when your child moves back home. Some parents choose not to charge their child rent, depending on the reason for moving home and whether they have a limited income due to unemployment or student status.

However, charging your child room and board, no matter how little, can help him learn to manage his finances and prepare him to live independently when he moves out. It might also reduce the chances of you becoming resentful if he is spending money elsewhere while depending on you.

At this age, your child should already be doing his own laundry and cleaning up after himself. In addition, asking him to contribute to general household chores, such as yard work, is reasonable.

If your child has to move home because he was laid off, it's easy to chalk his misfortune up to a bad economy. But if your child is employed, living at home, and not contributing to household expenses or chores, you might be enabling his dependency by being too accommodating. This isn't doing either one of you any favours. Learn when to draw the line and recognize that teaching independence is part of your role as a parent.

How long your child lives at home is dependent on his situation. If he is in school, you may want to set a move-out date a month or two after graduation. If your child is unemployed, expecting him to diligently look for a job, and move out upon employment, is reasonable. Have a discussion with your child and agree on a time frame. This will help him on his road to independence, and it will give you peace of mind knowing your child's situation isn't permanent.

As your child grows year by year and makes the transition from being a child to being a teenager, it's likely that they'll also experience some changes in their relationship with siblings too.

Having siblings is great for children, especially if they're relatively close in age or share interests. Although there may have been some degree of squabbling and falling out at times, which is only normal, many siblings do get on well together, enjoying company when playing games or having someone to boss around!

Same sex siblings may enjoy sharing toys or accessories, such as hair clips and bags, and may share friends too. But as children get older, it's only natural that their relationships with their siblings undergo some changes, especially as they enter the teenage years.

What Changes Might Occur?

For a teenager, one of the biggest changes occurring for them, and not for younger siblings, is a change in their hormones. As well as experiencing changes in their body, their hormones are raging, which can affect their mood. Whilst they may have previously been happy to tolerate and play with younger siblings, when they enter the teenage years, they may be less likely to want to.

For younger siblings, it's hard to suddenly find that a long-term playmate is no longer happy to cooperate with games. But it's not always a teenager's fault that they don't feel happy to do so, as their hormones can affect their mood and they may be grumpier than usual.

During the somewhat turbulent teenage years, it's also common for teenagers to reassess their views and opinions, often trying out new ideas and developing new aspects to their personality. These are all positive changes, but can come as a surprise and often a disappointment for younger siblings, who just want the same old sibling to remain, rather than a new, improved or different one.

Where they may previously have spent lots of time with the rest of the family, a teenager may now value their privacy and want to spend more time on their own, which can also be hard for a younger child too. Plus, who they want to spend time with may differ, as where they were previously happy to spend time with younger friends of the brother or sister, they may now exclusively want to be with people their own age. All of these changes can be hard on a younger sibling, who's grown up having an older brother or sister to play with in the evenings and weekends.

What Can You Do?

As a parent, you can do your best to help both parties by trying to explain the changes that are occurring. For example, if you're talking to the younger sibling you can chat about what's going on with their teenage sibling, emphasising that it's not anything they've done that has changed their brother or sister, but is just part of growing up. It's good to discuss the importance of letting them have their own space when they want it, but that they'll still be there for them sometimes. Teenagers may need a reminder now and then to remember the feelings of their younger siblings too. It's all too easy to be totally caught up in their experiences and forget or overlook the feelings of their family. Remind them that their younger sibling would like to spend some time with them too, misses their company and doesn't understand what the teenager is going through.

Above all, as parents, you can be there to support all your children, whatever their age and whatever experiences they're going through. Having support is one of the crucial elements that helps everyone through new and difficult times.

Many of us live in what we believe to be a completely heterosexual world, where gays and lesbians are simply people on television. We're wrong, of course. Everywhere we go, every single day, there are gays and lesbians; we simply don't realise it. There's nothing obvious to mark them out, and for the most part we can interact with them and never tell – and it really doesn't matter.

But how would you feel if one of those gays or lesbians was your teen? Given that the incidence of homosexuality is believed to be about one in ten, it could be. If you found that out, what would you do and how would you feel?

Is My Teen Gay?

Beyond inclinations towards the same sex, there may be no obvious markers that your teen will be a gay or lesbian. Even then, because of societal conditioning, for a number of the teenage years they might live a very straight life, even dating the opposite sex, until they find themselves – they might not even completely realise they're gay until they're older.

One thing you can do, if it's possible, is to voice approval of homosexuality. That way, if your teen is gay, he will feel more comfortable discussing it and opening up to you. The louder your disapproval, the more firmly that closet door will stay closed, and you'll be cut off from an important part of your child – their sexuality.

Coming right out and asking might bring a truthful answer, if the atmosphere at home seems accepting. But be wary of it as a tactic. If you discover, for instance, that your teen has been visiting gay or lesbian websites or porn sites, it's a strong indicator they may have gay feelings. Be very careful of confronting them with it, but edge around the subject, and give them the opportunity to open up – if they wish.

With younger teens, sometimes just asking can be the best way, especially if you have a good bond. If they do tell you, it gives you more chance to protect them (and for them to protect themselves) from the homophobia they'll encounter.

How Do You Accept It?

If you really love your teen, accepting them as they are should be natural, although it might take some time for you to come to terms with this discovery. Remember, they're still the same, and so are you. All that's changed is that they've trusted you with a piece of knowledge.

It can be a shock for you, and it can take you time to come to terms with it. That's fine. Take the time. The one thing you can't ever do is reject your teen for their sexual orientation. They are who they are. Don't write it off as just a phase. Accept it. You might have to ask them to limit their behaviour with dates around you, for instance (and treat their dates as you would a heterosexual date), but be actively there for them. Should They Come Out?

Coming out is a major step for anyone, but especially for a teen. It takes a lot of courage and a leap of faith. You have to stand with them and help them. Do you tell others in the family? The answer is no, not unless the teen allows it. Who knows has to be for them to decide?

They may feel their peers will be accepting of the fact, and if they're deciding whether to come out at school, you'd better sit and talk to them. Other teens can be very unforgiving, and there's a good chance they'll face harassment and bullying if they openly declare themselves to be gay. It shouldn't happen, of course, but it does. Urge them to think long and hard first, but if it's something they feel they have to do, make sure you offer very active support.

If they run into problems, take their side, and, if they want you to, contact the school and demand it takes action. If your teen approves, it could be useful to also contact the head teacher and tell them of your teen's sexual orientation, something they can share with a few trusted teachers. It could end up defusing situations at school.

Will other member of the family understand? Some will, others…well, perhaps some won't. Not everyone has to be told, by any means. Obviously, if the immediate family knows it's for the best, including brothers and sisters, but beyond that, you and your teen should discuss whether it's necessary at this point to tell certain relatives who might have homophobic views

Relationships

Sooner or later your teen is going to discover the opposite sex. If you're lucky, it will come later, so they can enjoy childhood a little while longer, but it will inevitably come.

And with it there will be all the problems of rejection, first love, romance, break up and finding someone new. It's an adventure, but for them one that's especially steeped in emotion as their hormones fly all over the place.

It will also be a time of sexual exploration, and that can be especially worrying for a parent – particularly the parents of a teen girl.

How do you cope with it all?

First Love
The first serious boyfriend or girlfriend is a major milestone in life, one they'll remember all through the years, usually with fondness. But it can also be a traumatic time, especially if they're part of a couple that constantly breaks up and gets back together.

All too often, advice is the last thing they want. Each generation thinks it's invented love and romance, and that parents simply can't understand – when you can, and all too well, of course. The best course is to offer advice only if they come to you, but be open to discuss what's happening in their romantic lives, especially during the bad times.

A break up can seem devastating, especially if the couple has been going out for a while (and remember that to teens, six months can seem like an eternity). Be there to console, to listen, and simply generally offer comfort. Your teen will be down and need the closeness of family even more than before.

Finding Someone
For all they love new things, teens can be great traditionalists in some ways. There are exceptions, of course, but usually boys ask girls out, and not the other way round. But some girls won't be asked, some boys won't have the courage to ask, and others will be rejected.

If there's trauma in romance, there's even more in no romance. The teens feel like failures if they're not asked, and failures if they ask and are rejected. The problem is that there's nothing practical you can do to help them, and you need to tread very carefully so you don't bruise already fragile egos. Be supportive, and give them lots of positive comments about their appearance, attitude and skills. It won't make up for them not having someone, but it might take their minds off it for a while.

Sex

Teens and sex...it's a minefield. These days they receive the lectures in school from an early age. But there's a big gap between theory and practice, and that's where you come in. You might not be able to control when your teen starts experimenting with sex, but you can give them encouragement not to begin too early, to start with someone they really like, and, above all, to be sensible about it and use protection.

The talks might be embarrassing for both you and your teen, but they're worthwhile if they prevent pregnancy, disease and heartbreak.

On a practical level, you can make sure that your teen – whether boy or girl – carries condoms, and in a gentle way try to drill it into them that they use them. Teens don't have the experience to believe bad things can happen to them; remind them that they do.

Some parents will preach abstinence, and some teens will follow that. It's fine. What's important is that they start when they're ready, not because of peer pressure or because sex seems so casual these days. You can try and ensure that they don't feel exploited. The more confident they are in themselves, the less likely they'll be to have sex too early.

Friendships

As your child grows into a teen and becomes more and more his or her own person, the circle of friends around him is probably going to change. Some old ones will be dropped and new ones taken up. Your teen will run with different crowds. The problem, of course, is that you might not like some of their new friends – it could be for a variety of reasons. In some cases it might well be more than just dislike, you might find them to be a bad influence.

But what can you do about a teen's friends?

Don't Voice Disapproval

The worst thing you can do is to criticise your teen's friends. Given the moody, contrary nature of teens, which is really only their way of becoming more independent, you'll just drive them all closer together.

That doesn't mean you have to approve of them, by any means. But if at all possible, learn to keep your mouth closed on the matter; it'll save a lot of arguments. If asked, give your opinion judiciously – don't provoke things, but there are still ways you can make it clear you don't approve.

The chances are that your teen will try on different sets of friends through these years, learning what works and what doesn't, so silence can be the best course. Often, like a phase, these friends will pass.

Certainly you shouldn't say anything if your teen starts dressing like a Goth or punk and takes up with similar people. Again, it's a costume. Inside the teen remains the same person, just with black nail polish and stranger clothes. See them for who they are, and the same applies to their friends. They're all just kids, growing up rapidly and trying to find their way and their place in the world.

Don't try and steer them in particular directions. Asking why they don't invite an old friend round any more can be seen a form of subtle pushing, and it won't work; they have to make their own decisions a lot of the time. Do encourage them to have new friends over, though. Not only does it give you the chance to meet them, but it makes your teen feel more accepted at home, in a time when feeling alienated is common.

When You Worry About Friends

The problem will come if you believe your teen's friends are leading them into bad habits – maybe drugs, maybe crime, or excessive drinking. At that point you feel you need to intervene, but doing so is going to cause a fracture between you.

Remember, your teen has a whole life ahead. If these problems are new, doing something about it now can leave a clear path in front of them. Wait too long and it could become too late. You have their welfare to put first. Even if it does cause arguments, you're doing it for their welfare, not your own.

How do you achieve it, though? You can try reason and conversation. In some cases that will work, but in many more, you might as well be talking to yourself. Grounding your teen might be effective with a few, but again, many will simply defy the ban, making things worse.

If you truly believe things are bad, to the point of danger, then get help to intervene. In the case of crime, talk to the police. It won't be easy, but they should be able to offer advice, or even do something themselves. In other cases, counselling can offer a solution.

It's a difficult choice to make, of course, but if you truly feel it's necessary, don't hesitate. In the long run, your teen may well thank you.

Teens can go through troubled and turbulent times and it's not unusual for teens to run away from home. It can be a stressful time for parents, who are left wondering what they can do best to help their teen. We explore practical ways of dealing with and helping teens who run away.

Sometimes problems at home or school, peer pressure or other worries just get too much and the only way out they can see is to run away. Sadly, it generally doesn't solve the problem and ends up creating more, although it can serve as a way for a teen to highlight just how bad about something they're feeling and when they come home, steps can be taken to resolve it.

What to Do When Your Teen Runs Away

Having a teen that runs away from home can be a very stressful and worrying time for parents, especially if you've got no idea where your teen has gone or why. Although it can be hard to understand or accept what has happened, especially if you were unaware there were any problems, you need to try and remain as calm as possible.

In the very first instance, if you're concerned about the whereabouts of your teen, then you should try and establish where the may have gone and if anyone knows where they are. For example, you could call and speak to all their friends, any relatives and anyone else who knows your teen and, if necessary, go out and look for them (but take your phone, in case they call). You may also need to phone the police.

Your teen's room

Your teen's room would probably normally be their own private space, but in this type of situation, especially if you've got no idea why they've run away or where they are, then having a quick look in their room may offer some clues. In particular, see if they've left any notes behind, written anything in a diary, received or sent relevant emails recently or even left their phone behind. To help find out who your teen may have called recently, then looking at their phone records may help.

Whilst Your Teen is Away

As parents, it's natural for you to blame yourself for your teen's disappearance and think it's something you've done wrong. Whatever the problem and reason for them running away, at this stage, there is no point blaming yourself. You've got to concentrate on working hard to find them and bring them home again.

When Your Teen Comes Home

In the large majority of cases, teens that have run away from home do come back again. Initially you may feel very relieved that they are back. Or you may feel angry at your teen for putting you through the stress of it, but put these feelings aside and focus on the fact that they are now home. It may help to give your teen some space at first, to recover from their experience and settle back in again at home. However, there is no doubt a reason behind their disappearance and you have to talk about this. Ignoring it and brushing it under the carpet is not a long term or practical solution and runs the risk of the problem arising again in the future.

If your teen does not feel comfortable talking to you about it, then find someone else that they will talk to – family, friends or a professional. Depending on what the problem is, you or they will need to find a way of working through them and, if necessary, seek extra help.

Above all, do let your teen know that you love them, care for them and want them to be safe and happy at all times.

Bullying

Many parents fear their children being bullied, but few even like to think about their child being a bully. The fact of the matter is, however, that any teenager could be a bully. Bullies can be boys or girls, may have been bullied or never been involved in bullying previously, and may bully by teasing or by violence. There are many different types of bullying and those who do bully have often been the victims of abuse themselves. If you suspect your teen is a bully, speak with school officials to find out the full story, discuss these behaviours with your teenager, and try to spend more time with you teenager at this difficult time.

Speak with School Officials

If you suspect, or are notified, that your teen is a bully then you need to find out the full story. What has your teen been doing? Who has your teen been doing it to? Has your teen been named as a bully by another teen or has an adult noticed his or her behaviours? Is there a particular pattern to the bullying? By finding out as many details as possible about you teen's behaviour you can begin to piece together an idea of what (s)he is doing and why (s)he is doing it. However, you'll only really be able to understand why bullying has begun by speaking about it with your teen.

Discuss Bullying with Your Teen

Funny enough, some teens may not even realise that they are bullying others. Many have become so used to seeing inappropriate behaviour around them or in society that they believe some actions, such as teasing others, are completely normal. Other actions, such as if a teen cheats on school work or engages in abuse or violence, are more obviously wrong. Many teens engage in bullying because they were bullied themselves or because they feel insecure or have low self-esteem. Only by discussing bullying with your teen can you be certain of why this behaviour has begun.

Spend More Time with Your Teenager

"Bully" is a term that means different things to different people, but if you spend more time with your teen then you will have ample opportunity to let him or her know exactly what it means for your family. Spending more time with your teen will also allow you to work on building up his or her self-esteem and model the kind of behaviour that you would like him or her to exhibit. This time together should be consistent and perhaps even private, so that teens don't feel that they need to share you (or your attention) with siblings or other people.

Parenting often brings a number of surprises and finding out that your teen is a bully may well be one of them. If you do discover that your teen is bullying others, be sure to speak with school officials to find out exactly what is happening, discuss the situation with your teen and spend more time with your teen to help him or her gain self-confidence and watch you model appropriate behaviour. If you do not feel that you are making progress on your own then enlisting the aid of a professional counsellor or therapist may also be a good idea.

Computers

Computers, especially those with an Internet connection, have become a part of modern life. Every day teens use them to do homework, research, keep in touch with friends, listen to music, watch television programmes and movies and generally entertain themselves. But when is enough enough?

How do you know if your teen has a healthy interest in electronics or has become addicted to the computer? Continue reading for some clues to help you determine if your teen's computer use has become addictive.

Time

One of the first things to think about in relation to a teen's computer use is how much time (s)he spends on the computer each day. This will obviously vary per person, but in general if a teen is spending more than an hour or two on the computer then it is likely that (s)he is missing out on other parts of life. Also think about the time of day that a teen is on the computer. If a teen comes home from school and heads to the computer to do homework this is one thing, but if a teen waits until the family has gone to bed to begin his or her computer use then it is quite another.

Purpose

Do you know why your teen is using the computer? If you ask your teen, will (s) he tell you? These are two questions that any parent should be asking in regards to teen computer use. As a general rule of thumb, teens who can immediately and articulately describe why they use the computer usually do have a reason to be on them. However, teens that are vague or secretive about their computer use may have no reason to be on the computer other than because they are addicted or fear living their life away from the machine.

Other Activities

In addition to using the computer, can you think of activities that your teen enjoys and engages in regularly? If so, then it is likely that your teen has a fairly balanced life. If not, then it is likely that your teen is sacrificing or otherwise missing out on a well rounded life for the sake of spending time on the computer. Though extra computer use may be acceptable at certain times (for example, during school holidays), in general it should not take up so much time that it precludes a teen from engaging in other activities.

Friends

Electronic communication has become a way of life for teens, from sending text messages to instant messaging to sending emails. However, there is a difference between electronic communication that complements face-to-face communication and electronic communication that is used instead of face-to-face communication. Talk to your teen about his or her friends. Are they available in real life or do you have a sneaking suspicion that your teen has only online friends? Do you think your teen is following proper Internet safety methods or do you fear that (s)he may be disclosing sensitive information to these new friends? Does your teen ever meet his or her friends off line? Is this a common occurrence? The more you ponder your teen's friendships the more you may realise about his or her computer use.

In general, teens love technology and a computer has become a fact of life for these youngsters. If you fear that your teen has become addicted to the computer, think about the time (s)he spends on it, the purpose for which (s)he logs on, if (s)he engages in other activities and who (s)he counts as friends. These variables usually give parents a well-rounded picture of a teen's computer use and enough information to decide if their teen seems to be addicted to the computer.

Teenagers need to do chores. As teenagers navigate their way from childhood to adulthood they need to learn to take on more responsibilities and contribute to their own household. Not only do household chores allow an adolescent to be in control of something and learn how to take responsibility for his or her actions, but they teach him or her important life skills that will be needed when he or she is running a household in the future. Most chores that teenagers do well with are associated with cooking and housework.

Teenagers and Responsibility

Teenagers learn from having responsibilities of their own. This does not mean that teenagers will not make mistakes and act irresponsibly, but learning from these mistakes is an important way for teens to understand the impact that their actions can have and why being responsible is necessary when people depend upon each other. Parenting, then, requires adults to step back and allow teenagers to fail or succeed with their responsibilities on their own. If teens seem to fail more often then not, then discussing their responsibilities and finding out why they are having trouble is important. When parents and teens are on the same page regarding what it takes to be successful the chances of this occurring will rise.

Teenagers and Cooking

Many parents do not want their children to cook on their own and this is understandable. However, teenagers are not children. Once teens have been taught proper kitchen safety and basic recipes, encouraging them to explore good nutrition and their culinary talents will help them feel comfortable in the kitchen before they need to fend for themselves all the time. To this end, expecting teens to prepare the menu for, and cook, a meal a week is a good idea. Many teens will be pressed for time and money so allowing them to add their needed ingredients to the family shopping list is smart, but expecting them to work within budgetary constraints and dietary guidelines will help them become familiar with these obstacles early on. After a few months teens will likely be able to count cooking as one of their talents and the family will hopefully begin to enjoy a range of new dishes on teen cooking nights.

Teenagers and Housework

Most teenagers do chores around the house. Keeping their own bedrooms clean, changing and washing their linens, doing their own laundry, pitching in with the ironing, helping to keep common areas neat, taking out the rubbish bins and sorting recycling materials are all chores that teens are more than qualified for which to take responsibility. Parents should be careful to maintain that chores are a teen's responsibility, however, and not descend to bribing or rewarding teens for taking care of the chores that they should be completing as a matter of course. Keeping a chore chart may help everyone in the family remember what needs to be done, but awarding teens stickers or stars might be seen as too babyish for teens. Teens learn responsibility and life skills from completing household chores. Expecting your teen to complete consistent chores will help the whole family maintain take responsibility for keeping a lovely home.

Single Parent

It's difficult being a single parent. When your children are young, though, they tend to respond more easily to a parent. In adolescence, though, they want to spread their wings more and gain more independence. That may mean an especially tough time for a single parent, the only symbol of authority in the home.

Some studies have shown that teens from single-parent households can show a greater rate of delinquency and tend not to do as well at school, although always it's dependent on the familial relationship – generalisations are just that, and statistics can be made to say different things.

How can single parents cope with teens?

The Bond

One advantage single parents often enjoy is a tight bond with their children. The child has been forced to rely on one parent, and is often more open with them than they might be with both a father and mother around.

That can help during the teenage years, making it easier to discuss more delicate issues and address problems as they arise. Of course, identifying those problems can become harder. A single parent is likely to be at work all day, and with the teen gone more than a younger child, there's less contact, so you might not know as much of what's going on in your teen's life.

Communicate as much as possible, and use that bond to remain close if you can. It's natural for teens to talk less about their lives as they grow older, but encourage it.

The Ex

In many cases, your ex will have stayed close to the teens, even if the things they share are different to you and the teen. Where you have a good relationship with your ex, don't be afraid to call and discuss issues involving the child and develop a strategy between the two of you – it certainly stops the teen playing one parent against the other, and means you show an important united front. After all, you both love your child and want the best for him or her.

If relations aren't so good, but your ex still sees the teen regularly, that can cause problems. You won't know what's happening on visits. All you can do is encourage good communication with your teen. If serious problems arise, contact your ex and see if the two of you can work together to help your teen.

Problem Behaviour

Teens rebel against parents, it's the way of the world. But if you're a single parent, you're the constant target of rebellion, and it can become both wearing and stressful; there's no down time where another parent can take over.

As much as you can, you need to be constantly vigilant, so you're aware early of any trouble with drink, drugs or other things. That doesn't necessarily mean spying, unless you really suspect something's wrong, but you have to keep a detachment to see your teen as objectively as possible.

Praise the good things, and try to discuss areas that concern you, but without being openly critical, unless the behaviour is unacceptable or worries you. Empathise as much as possible (you probably remember being a teen yourself) and try to see things from their point of view.

Talk to other parents, gather their views – a problem shared can really seem like a problem halved, and other might have excellent advice. If you have good friends of the opposite sex that your teen trusts, bring them in and have them talk to the teen. Use the resources available to you that can help both you and your teen.

Staying over at friends

When you're child becomes a teen, sleepovers involving a couple of classmates, a big bowl of popcorn and some cartoon-covered sleeping bags have become a thing of the past. Unfortunately sleepovers can take a more sinister turn during the teen years with many teenagers using them as cover to stay out late, experiment with alcohol and/or drugs, and host members of the opposite sex in their bedrooms. However, this does not mean that your teen will engage in these activities nor that you must ban sleepovers entirely to avoid them. Instead, simply discuss house rules regarding sleepovers with your teen and make sure that everyone involved understands the expectations for the next time their friends decide to stay at your home.

Invited Guests

One of the first house rules that parents should discuss with their teens regarding sleepovers is about invited guests. Are there any specific individuals who are not allowed to stay the night in your home? Are members of the opposite sex allowed to stay the night in your home? How many invited guests are allowed to stay the night in your home at any one time? Will invited guests need to prove to you that their parents know where they are for the night? These are all questions that parents of teens must consider before allowing their teen to invite friends over for a sleepover.

Acceptable Activities
While it's highly unlikely that today's teens would plan to gather 'round the piano for a sing-a-long during a sleepover, it's best if you discuss what are acceptable activities when there are guests staying the night. Are there any areas of the home that will be off limits to guests? Are there any items or possessions that you do not want guests handling? Is there a certain time when they must shut off the television/computer/games console? How do you feel about telephone calls from/to either your house phone or your teen's mobile? Many of these rules will likely conform to the house rules you keep anyway, but it's best to remind teens of them before each sleepover.
Food and Beverages
When teens have friends staying the night its pretty normal for them to expect to pig out on ice cream and crisps, but are there any food or drink items that you would not want your teen offering? To begin with, discuss your policies on alcohol (and illegal drugs), particularly if you keep a stocked bar in your home. Also consider discussing who will buy food and beverages for the sleepover (is it part of your housekeeping budget or will it come from your teen's spending money?), where it will be stored (in your teen's room or with the family

supplies?), and if there are any items that can not be taken during a sleepover (the ingredients for tomorrow's dinner, for example). Also consider discussing take-away and delivery options with your teen so that you won't be awakened at 3am wondering if they really were just getting some chips…

Logistics
Finally, discuss the logistics of a sleepover with your teen before each sleepover. Who will be picking up and dropping off the guest? Are they expecting to leave your home at any time, and if so how do they plan to get there? Will you expect them to be home by a certain hour? Will you expect them to be in bed by a certain hour? Where will they sleep? Will you require them to be awake by a certain hour? Is there are certain time by which guests must leave the next day? While these rules may change depending upon the situation, it is best for teens to know of your expectations before each sleepover so that there are no hurt feelings or shocked surprises while you have a guest in your home.

Party at your home

At some point or other, the chances are that your teen will host a party at your house. It might happen with your permission, or it could occur when you're on holiday somewhere, leaving your teen home alone and faced with the temptation of having friends over, and the first you learn is when you come home.

There have been news stories about teens posting details of their parties on social networking sites, leading to hundreds of gatecrashers and thousands of pounds worth of property damage, a scary thought for any parent.

It's natural for a teen to want to have a party, if only to pay back for all the others they attend. But is it possible to have a reasonable teenage party?

Trust

Trust between you and your teen is vital in many areas, and that includes a party. It's much better that you give your permission and know its happening than having the news arrives as a shock later.

If your teen wants a party one weekend, talk about it. With those fifteen or older, it's certainly best if you're not around, but with younger ones having at least one parent there unobtrusively can be a good idea.

If you're going on holiday and leaving your older teen at home, discuss whether they can have a party, and if so, when. But whatever the circumstances, you need to lay down some rules, and discuss the reasons behind them. Additionally, pack away all valuable and breakable items, just to be sure they're safe!

Perhaps the most important rule is that the party isn't advertised anywhere. Friends are welcome, and there will probably be unknown friends of friends who arrive, but set limits on the numbers.

A party isn't a party without music, but there are the neighbours to consider. Have your teen – not you – visit the houses on either side to explain they're having a party and that there will be loud music, but that it will be turned down by, say, midnight at the latest; that's simple courtesy. You certainly don't want the police called out because of the volume.

Alcohol

What about drink? Older teens are going to drink, and there's no way around that. But with younger teens, having a parent on the premises means that any attempts to smuggle alcohol in can be thwarted. With older teens – those of legal drinking age - you might consider supplying some beer as well as soft drinks and snacks – for younger, the same but without the beer.

Teenagers are discovering sex, and a party can be an ideal atmosphere for further exploration, especially after a few drinks. Obviously, you can't eliminate it, but do all you can to discourage it. Making the bedrooms off-limits – locking them if need be – certainly helps. No one can guarantee it won't happen, since where there's a will, there's a way, but you can make it more difficult.

With drugs, there's one simple answer – no. If other teens want to take drugs, there's little you can do about it, but impress on your teen that you won't tolerate it in your house, and make sure they impress that on their friends.

Gatecrashers and Violence

People gatecrash parties, and if your teen isn't the one answering the door, they often get in. It's not an ideal situation, but it happens and there's little to be done about it, unless they cause trouble.

Violence, too, can occur. In both instances, unless it can be quickly defused, encourage your teen to call the police. It's better to have them there, taking care of things, before events escalate to tragedy.

Point out to your teen that having a party means responsibility, that you expect them to act responsibly and if they don't, you'll take appropriate measures. At the same time, if something happens that's beyond their control, don't penalise them for it.

Well planned, parties can be wonderful, and bring great memories for your teen. Work with them to do all you can to make sure that happens – you might even be willing to let them have another one!

Money

We all need money for things, as that applies to your teen every bit as much as it does to you. The difference, though, is where you work to earn yours, all too often your teen is reliant on you and the pocket money you supply.

Obviously, there's no fixed amount you should give. A lot depends, for a start, on how much you can afford, and what else you give them – do you buy all their clothes and shoes, for instance? In return for pocket money, what should you expect, or should it be given no matter what?

Some Basic Rules

While kids have grown up receiving pocket money every week, by the time they're teens they want to be seen as adults. You can just continue giving them money, but it's also a good idea to begin instilling a sense of responsibility in them, and to let them know, now they're older, that you don't receive something for nothing.

Set a list of weekly chores they have to perform to earn their pocket money. It doesn't have to be pages long, or particularly complex. You might include something like taking out (and bringing back in!) the bins, emptying the rubbish and cleaning their rooms. It needn't take long, but it's something less for you – although you might have to remind them – and involves them more in the running of the household.

There are some who would link pocket money to behaviour. It can be understandable with teens who've become a bit unruly, and certainly this carrot approach, rewarding good behaviour, has its points, but it's also a stick. However, it's probably only worth considering as a disciplinary measure if you really have a problem, and some advocates would say don't link the two at all.

Teens like to go out, and at times they'll want extra money. It's not a good idea to sub them an advance on pocket money. A far more constructive idea is to let them do jobs to earn it. They can mow the grass, weed the flowerbeds, wash the car, all those tasks you've been meaning to do but haven't found the time to accomplish. Set a fair rate of pay beforehand, but tell them you expect the job done properly. They might grumble, but there will be no complaints when they're paid.

Pocket Money and Saturday Jobs
When they're old enough, some teens will start working. Some will have paper rounds; others will take on Saturday jobs. They'll be earning their own money, but most will still feel they should be receiving pocket money from you, just as they always have.
It's a delicate issue. Since it promotes discipline and responsibility, you want to encourage the work ethic (as long as it doesn't interfere with school and homework, of course). At the same, when they're earning more than they were receiving from you, you might wonder whether you should continue giving pocket money. Sit down and discuss it – especially if your own finances are tight. See if you can arrange a compromise, perhaps with you paying for more things, while they use their earnings for items they want. Encourage saving. In all probability, they won't receive enough pocket money to save any of it, but suggest saving at

least part of their birthday and Christmas money, and part of whatever wages they earn.

When to Stop Pocket Money
As all parents know, pocket money never really stops. You'll remain the bank of parent, giving loans and gifts of cash for years to come. But once they begin work full-time or go on to university, the official weekly payment should cease. They're fully adult at that point, and by removing the support, you're acknowledging that they're old enough to stand on their own two feet.

Teenagers Bedroom

What is it about teens and cleaning their rooms? Yes, some do a great job, keeping everything impeccably, scarily neat, but the vast majority don't seem to care. Boys are probably worse than girls, but plenty of both sexes seem content to live for a few years in a pigsty with clothes and everything else thrown all over the place.
You want them to keep their rooms somewhat tidy – before it becomes a health hazard – so how do you get them to actually perform the task? It helps if they've been encouraged to it from an early age, but even those good habits can fall by the wayside in adolescence.
However, there are certain things you should be able to expect – and you should be willing to forgive a certain amount of clutter; after all, it's a teen's room, not a barracks.

What to Expect
It's worth laying down some basic rules for your teen about what's acceptable in keeping the room clean. Point out, first of all, that they're only responsible for their own room, not the whole house. Tell them that you'll supply clean sheets, but

they should be changed weekly, and that you expect the floor to be litter-free.

Eating in the room is fine, with the provision that all dirty dishes have to be returned to the kitchen on a daily basis. As to laundry, be willing to wash it as long as they bring it down – provide a laundry basket for them – and they have to put away their clean, folded clothes. After the first time they run out of clean clothes, they'll never forget again!

That gives them responsibility, but also a certain level of independence, which is important in the teenage years, and their room should rightly be largely their domain. It also takes the onus off you, but don't remind or nag them about things unless it's absolutely necessary.

What do you do, though, with those who simply won't do what's expected? You have two possibilities – the carrot and the stick.

The Carrot

It can be much better to praise, or even bribe, your teen into cleaning his room than exerting discipline, which becomes another conflict at a time that's full of them. Offering chore money often works well, especially when the teen is broke; just don't be extravagant.

When a room's been cleaned, praise them for a job well done, and make them feel proud of it (in reality it might not be much, but make them feel as if it is). Positive reinforcement can be a surprisingly powerful tool. Offer to take them shopping for something for the room if they'll clean it first. That's especially useful when they've had their eye on a small piece of furniture or a poster.

The Stick

Berating a teen for constantly failing to clean his room simply isn't productive. You might well hear, "It's my room," and when you respond "It's my house and my rules," all that's going to happen is an argument, which does no one any good. But there are things you can do. Refuse to give pocket money until the job has been done, or, if they're hoping for a lift somewhere, refuse because they haven't done as agreed – and don't be put off with "I'll do it when I get home"; that rarely turns into fact.

Threaten those kinds of punishments as a last resort. But if you do threaten, always follow through if they don't clean their rooms. Leave the threat empty, and the room will stay dirty.

At some point your teen will blurt out that life isn't fair. They're right, of course, it isn't, but it might well be worth pointing out to them that no one ever claimed it was. What they'll find, once they're out and on their own is that they have to look after themselves - no one will put hot meals on the table for them, run them hither and yon or do their laundry. But one thing you can do for your teen before they leave the nest is teach them how to look after themselves properly. You'll have more peace of mind after they're gone, knowing that at least they can cook a decent meal, and there might even be the added bonus that they'll help out around the house, although it's possibly better not to hold your breath on that one!

The Basics
The basics come down to cooking and cleaning. Although there's a move in schools to teach pupils how to cook, everyone knows there's no meal like the ones you get at home, and you know what your kids' favourites are.

Teach them how to prepare those dishes. Take them through each stage, step by step, first with them watching, then helping, then finally doing it themselves while you supervise - of course, this will take several sessions over a few weeks.

But do more besides. Show them how to cook bacon and eggs, for instance, or the right way to cook vegetables, the skills they'll need to survive in the kitchen. For good measure, show them how to wash up, too, explaining that's part of the cooking process.

You might even want to give them a basic cookery book so they can extend their range of dishes. Some will find they have a talent for cooking and take easily to it. Others won't, but as long as they can master the basics, they'll never starve or have to spend a fortune on ready meals.

Cleaning

Their rooms at home might look like tips, but any parent knows that when the kids move out they'll have to do more with their own places. Most of us take cleaning for granted, but it doesn't hurt to show teens the best way to dust and vacuum, and also how to give rooms like the kitchen and the bathroom a thorough clean.

It might take a while for them actually to do it, but knowing that they have the ability is a good start (and a gift of cleaning supplies and an old vacuum cleaner when they move out doesn't hurt, either, and serves as a good hint).

Laundry

Everyone needs clean clothes. Teens probably never consider the effort involved, but at some point they're going to have to learn the hard way. Teaching them how to do it right will stop phone calls wondering what to do when colours have bled into whites, and also means they won't be looking around for help in the launderette, or with the washing machine in a rented flat.

Some may never iron clothes, so at least show them how to fold things properly. Teaching them the proper way to iron, too, can be a plus, even if they never bother with the skill.

Chapter 24

Keeping teens safe Online

The Internet is a great technological invention, but despite its numerous positive benefits, there are dangers lurking too. Your teen will know doubt be using the Internet in some shape or form, so it's important to teach them about online safety.

It's a good idea to chat about the potential dangers of the Internet to your teen, so they understand why it's important to stay safe online. This doesn't necessarily mean a big scaremongering chat that will scare them away from ever wanting to log on (even if this means you could have more frequent access to your computer!) but a practical and thoughtful look at the dangers and why everyone should be wary and protect themselves.

Giving Out Personal Information Online
One of the issues to discuss is the type of information that should and shouldn't be given out online. Your teen may well use social networking sites such as Facebook or MySpace, write a blog or participate in chat forums. All of these methods of Internet use are great, but will encourage some degree of information sharing.

For example, Facebook and MySpace have sections where you can fill out a profile and give information about yourself, and for blogging or chatting on forums, you'll need a username and often have the chance to add in more details about yourself.

It's essential to instil in your teen the idea that it's not good to give out too many personal details about yourself, even if you think it's safe and only your friends will find it.

As a basic rule, you should never give out your full name, your address or your date of birth, as if these details fall into the wrong hands, they could be used to steal your identity. But teens should also be wary about giving out too many other details, like their phone number, where they go to school or college, who their friends are and where they live.

It's hard not to, when everyone else seems to be freely sharing these details, but you never know who could be looking at them (even your Facebook profile and photos aren't secure, unless you've set up privacy settings) or how they could be used, so for ultimate safety, it's best for teens to be wary about how much information they share about themselves online.

Who to Talk to Online

Likewise, there should be some reservations with who teens talk to online. Having an anonymous profile may seem like a good safety caution, but the trouble is that you never know if other people are being truthful about who they really are. For example, there have been many cases of adults masquerading as teens on online forums in order to befriend teens.

So although it's fine to chat to people on forums, if teens don't know who they're talking to, it's best to keep track on the public area of the forum and make sure they do not give out their email address, phone number or other means of contact to a faceless person who could be anyone.

Posting Photos Online

Another big issue that teens should be briefed about when keeping safe online is the issue of posting photos of themselves online.

These days there's a major trend amongst teens to post lots of photos of themselves and their friends on social networking sites such as Facebook. Although it seems harmless enough, as photos can be tagged with people's names, anyone could effectively find out who you are and what you look like, which really compromises online safety.

What's more, unless privacy settings have been implemented, even people your teen isn't friends with and doesn't know on Facebook could access pictures of them. It's hard to go against the trend, but your teen should be wary of posting too many photos of themselves online. Ideally, they should also discourage their friends from tagging them in their pictures, as this will slightly reduce ease of identification.

Facebook

The social networking site, Facebook, has soared in popularity in the last few years and is now used by millions of people around the world. A large number of its users are teens, who love to keep in touch with their friends, tell people what they're up to and share pictures and videos. Whilst it may seem harmless enough, there are potential risks involved, but there's plenty you can do, as parents, to help ensure your teens use Facebook safely.

"Everyone's on Facebook," is likely to be a comment your teen may have made in relation to the popular social networking site. It used to be MySpace or Bebo that generated all the interest, but Facebook has well and truly taken over in the popularity ranks.

The idea of social networking is great – you create your own page on the site where you can provide information about yourself, post pictures, let people know what you've been doing, and keep in contact with all your friends. With Facebook, there are lots of added extras too, so you can join groups that support causes you relate to, become fans of brands or people, join groups for your school or college, play games, fill in memes and send virtual gifts to your friends.

Hidden Dangers of Facebook

But amidst all the nice elements of Facebook, sadly there are dangers lurking too. There's often a tendency for teens to add anyone and everyone to their Facebook friends list, so in reality some of them might not be friends at all. Adding someone without adding privacy settings will mean that they can automatically see everything you've posted, all your pictures, your friends pictures where you've been tagged, all your videos, personal information, who you're friends with and your status updates.

Whilst most teens may not think twice about this, not everyone uses information in a positive way. Sometimes information or pictures may be copied and used in a malicious way (online bullying using social networking information is sadly becoming a common phenomenon) and if teens subsequently fall out with 'friends', their shared images or information may be used in a harmful way.
If they're making friends via Facebook, you don't always know who people really are or if they're who they say they are. For example, there may be older people masquerading as teens to try and befriend them or paedophiles lurking behind teen profiles.

Helping Your Teen Use Facebook Safely
As a parent, you can do a lot to help ensure your teen understands the potential dangers and learns to use Facebook safely.
Carefully explain the dangers to them, or ask an older sibling or friend to chat to them about it. For example, it's not advisable to put your whole name, date of birth, address and phone numbers on Facebook, as this gives too much information away (and it could be stolen). They should also think carefully about how much information they give away about themselves, their school and friends and where they live

in their profile. If they're not sure, then keep it simple, as true friends will know the details anyway.

In addition, do mention the dangers of posting slightly risqué photos on Facebook. Teens have a tendency to do this and although may seem fun at the time, in future this is the kind of photo they may regret – and once it's out in the public domain, anyone could see it or use it.

If you need to understand how things work yourself, then you could try setting up an account and having a play with the security settings. Although some teens are happy to be friends online with their parents, others might not be quite so comfortable with that – but it's not necessarily due to them wanting to hide things from you, it might just be as it's not 'cool' to be friends with your mum on Facebook!

Making Use of Facebook Privacy Settings

To help teens using Facebook to add more security to who views certain information, pictures or details about them, there are various privacy settings that you can make use of. Although they're not always that widely known about, you can find the relevant settings under 'Settings' and 'Privacy Settings' on the top right hand menu bar. They take a bit of setting up, but the privacy settings are great, as you can control who sees which bits of your profile, pictures, updates, videos, friends and any other information. You can also group your friends into certain categories, such as 'school friends', 'college friends' or 'acquaintances,' and automatically assign the same privacy settings to all the people on that list.

If your teen is adding new albums of photos, don't let them forget to add the security settings too. Some of the general privacy settings are quite loose on Facebook, meaning that anyone that clicks on a tagged photo of your teen in an album can look at all their pictures – even if they're not friends with them. This is one reason why teens should suggest to their friends that they increase their security settings too, as however careful they are, their friends may be less so.

If some teens had their way, they'd spend their entire day on the Internet. Whilst the Internet does offer a great way for them to do research for their school or college work, relax and catch up with their friends, should you monitor and keep tabs on your teen's Internet use?

Whether or not parents should monitor their teen's Internet use is a hotly debated issue and something that parents may be in two camps about. On the one hand, it's good for teens to be to use the Internet on their own and have their own degree of privacy in what they're doing.

But on the other hand, it's easy for them to get carried away, spend too much time online, view less than savoury material online, engage in reckless online activity or accidentally become in contact with people online who aren't who they say they are. It's for those types of reasons that some parents wonder if they should monitor their teen's Internet use.

How Could You Monitor Internet Use?

If you'd like to keep more of an eye on how your teen uses the Internet or how much they're using it, then there are several ways in which you can do so.

In the first instance, it's a good idea not to make too much of an issue of using the Internet, as this could cause a backlash in your teen and make them want to use it more! If you're worried about the online safety side of things, then it's useful to teach your teen about basic safety issues – such as not giving out too much personal information online, being wary of over-friendly strangers in chat rooms and not taking everything that people they don't know say at face value, as they may well be lying.

Whilst teens may yearn to have a computer in their bedroom, it can be easier to monitor usage if the computer is actually in a public part of the house, like in a corner of a room, in a hallway, in a study or even on the landing (if there's room!). That way, you can be going about your own tasks in the home and keep a watchful eye on how much your teen is using the Internet, without being overly nosey.

It's also worth considering whether to impose a time limit on Internet use. For example, have set times agreed when teens can go online to do research for homework, check Facebook or play online games, but stick to the timetabled arrangements and come offline when the time is up. Otherwise there's the temptation for them to get caught up online for hours at a time, which isn't healthy.

Checking Web History

It's not a good idea to constantly check up on what they're using on the Internet or to make a big deal of it, but if you're unsure about what they're doing, or think they're acting suspiciously when using the computer (for example suddenly switching screens when you walk past or stopping what they're doing when you're in the room), then you can always check the history in browsers, such as Internet Explorer, after they've come off the computer. This will give you a list of sites they've visited on a certain day or week.

If you have concerns about teens stumbling onto unsavoury websites, then there are special pieces of software you can install to block out access to certain sites. This may give some degree of piece of mind, but then there is the potential that curiosity might get the better of your teen and they look at the sites elsewhere on someone else's computer instead!

Whether or not you decide to monitor teen Internet usage is up to you and will no doubt vary from parent to parent, but the main thing is to ensure your teens are safe online and get the best out of their Internet usage.

As they move into the teenage years, it's not uncommon for your previously chatty and friendly child to transform into a surly and uncommunicative teenager. If you'd like to build up communication again, here are some ideas for encouraging your teenager to talk.

The teenage years can be difficult for parents in many ways, not least in the communication stakes, as teens are prone to becoming less communicative with their parents. Teenagers are inevitably going through a lot of changes themselves, including having heaps of hormones charging around their body, but it can be hard for parents who suddenly find that their previously happy to chat child no longer seems to want to talk to them.

This lack of communication is a relatively common trait with teenagers and is typically characterised by teens only muttering or murmuring replies in response to parental queries, speaking in monosyllabic answers or resorting to nodding or shaking their heads instead of proper answers. Gone will be the time when you knew what your child had done at school, what experiences they've had or who their latest friends are. At a time when you'd like to be part of your teen's life even more than ever, this can be really trying for parents to deal with.

There may well come a time when your teen wants to find a Saturday job, in order to earn some money. It could be in a supermarket, a shop, labouring on a building site over the summer or just a paper round.

It's a first step towards independence, to have an income that's not pocket money and controlled by you. But it also brings responsibility. They have to be at work for each and every shift, on time (and punctuality is especially important for a paper round).

But it can be a shock when your teen comes and says they'd like to start working part-time. They're growing up and away from you. What do you do in that situation?

Chapter 25

The Big Questions

Perhaps the most important question is whether a job will interfere with school work, because school has to be the priority. If the job is, literally, just Saturday, and they're old enough (from the age of 13 you're allowed to work a certain number of hours each week), and it can fit in with other plans, then there's no reason to say no – at least as long as the work is reasonable, the hours and pay fair, and everything is legal and above board.

However, be sure of all those factors first. Sit down and discuss things with your teen – what they'll be doing, where the job is, how they'll get there, how much they'll be getting paid. They might not even know! Before they agree to take the job, make sure they have all the details; you want to be certain they're not being exploited.

But what if the job includes some evening work, which can be the case with some supermarket jobs, for instance? That can easily impinge on homework time. If your teen is serious about taking the job, the two of you need to devise a schedule that allows for both. You need to stress, though, that you trust the teen to keep to the bargain and make sure the schoolwork is done before they leave for their job.

Paper rounds are a special case. They mean a commitment to working every morning or afternoon, whatever the weather, and your teen – it tends to be younger teens – might not understand exactly what's involved. Point out that it will take a special person to be up early every morning and out in the rain and snow delivering papers. They'll have to be self-disciplined – add the fact that this job is theirs, and in most instances they shouldn't be asking you to help.

When The Job Doesn't Work Out

Most of the time, there's no problem with balancing a job and school. Sometimes, though, for a number of different reasons, your teen might want to quit the Saturday job. It might not be the right job for them, or they'll feel too crowded for time, or simply be unhappy.

Sit down and discuss the reasons with them. If they're valid, not simply a passing dissatisfaction, then agree that leaving is a good idea. But insist they do it properly, by giving notice in writing and working out the full notice. Not only is that fair to the employer who took a chance on them in the first place, it helps them obtain a reference for the next job they seek. They might not be thinking that far ahead, but you should.

With a paper round, monitor your teen's performance. Do they seem especially sleepy, for example, and is it affecting their schoolwork? If the answers are yes, then they need to leave the job. Again, talk to them, point out that school comes first and the work is suffering. Talk to the newsagent, too. Your teen might insist that they can handle it, but if it's apparent that they can't, then you need to make them see that leaving is the right thing to do. In all probability, the first morning they don't have to be up early, they'll thank you!

Chapter 26

Taking Drugs

A number of teens do take drugs in Britain, and it's true that the country does have a drug problem among its young, whether it's using cannabis, sniffing glue or solvents, or taking pills of different kinds.

The good news is that it's nowhere near as endemic as many of the tabloid papers would have you believe. The majority of kids don't use drugs, and your teen might well be among them.

But if not, or even if you suspect not, it can be a nerve-wracking experience for parents. What do you do if your teen is taking drugs?

Are They Taking Drugs?

It can be difficult for parents to tell sometimes if their teens are using drugs. In many cases there are no immediate outward signs, and asking them isn't usually going to bring an admission. They know drugs are illegal and bad, so they're certainly not going to tell you.

However, it's worth remembering that there's a big difference between using drugs and being addicted to something. Even when teens try drugs, the number who go on to become regular users is small, and the percentage of addicts far tinier yet. However, that doesn't make it easier for parents. You don't want your kids even beginning to set foot on that road.

A lot try drugs because of peer pressure, others from low self-esteem or a sense of alienation, or simply because different heroes use them.

The signs of drug use can be similar to depression or moodiness, but if you find cigarette papers, pill bottles, foil, or anything that could be a homemade pipe around then you know your teen is using – and probably smoking pot. For

other drugs, other than heroin, you might not see any
paraphernalia.

What to Do
The first thing is not to panic. You heart might be beating fast,
but try not to worry. What you need to do is sit down and
have a gentle conversation with your teen. If you know
they're using something, don't rant and rave. Ask them why,
what they get from it they can't get from something else.
Don't feel as if you've failed as a parent; you haven't.
Explain that it worries and upsets you, that it's something you
can't understand and won't be able to grasp (if you've used
drugs in your younger years, as some parents will have done,
this approach won't work, of course – you'll need to explain
why you stopped and why you feel they're not good). Never
mind the illegality. Tell them you love them unreservedly, and
you want to work with them to stop them using drugs.
If your teen really is addicted to something, then you need to
act immediately. Talk to your GP and see what can be done
about getting your teen into rehab to break the habit. It won't
be easy, for you or them, but in the long run the results will
far outweigh the pain.
Talking To Your Teen About Drugs
Your teen might well be better informed about drugs than you
are. But if you can stop them wanting to take drugs before
they even begin, that's the best course. Sit them down and talk
about drugs and their effects. If you've used drugs yourself in
the past, be wary of admitting it, as they might see it as
permission to experiment – if it was good enough for you, it's
fine for them – even though the times and circumstances were
different. Point out that it's not just illegal drugs that are bad.
What about all those energy drinks and tablets, and even the
effects of prescription drugs. Make it a wide-ranging talk that
covers all the bases. Encourage questions. If you don't know
the answers, find them and talk more.

Drugs can ruin lives. In most cases, they won't, but if you can stop the possibility of it happening to your teen by talking and loving them, isn't it worthwhile?

Chapter 27

Gangs,

Everyone will agree, are a blight on modern life. Originally an American problem, they've mushroomed over here, especially in the inner cities. According to a Channel 4 study, there are children as young as five years old joining gangs, and half the gun killings and fully a quarter of gun crimes in the UK in 2007 could be attributed to those under 18. Knife crime, especially among teens, has soared, and innocent teens can be attacked for simply walking harmlessly in the wrong postcode if a gang controls it.

That's very worrying for parents of teens. With the number of gangs and the level of violence escalating almost every week, it seems, what can you do?

Is Your Teen In A Gang?

It's a question most parents don't even want to contemplate, let alone ask. But many are, and not just boys, but girls, too. If your teen's school work has gone downhill, if they're staying out later and won't say where they've been, don't want to introduce you to their friends and seem to have undergone a change of attitude, becoming harder, more aloof and less friendly, there's the possibility they might be a gang member – or crew, as they're often known. In some instances particular items of clothing can identify gang members.

Not all who act that way are, of course – it could just be a teenage phase. But the best way to find out is simply to come out and ask. Some will be proud of the fact and flaunt it.

Others, naturally, will deny it all, in which case you'll need to do a little detective work to discover the truth.

If they are gang members, you need to lay the unglamorous truth about gangs out before them, the statistics on violence and death – the figures are terrifying, and quite easy to find. Tell them, quite bluntly, that you won't tolerate any gang insignias or behaviour in the house. Be plain that you won't tolerate knives or guns in the house, either, even if they claim they need them for protection.

The problem, of course, is that they might just hide the weapons outside the house, and there's little you can do about that. Try to discover why they joined a gang. It could be to belong; it could be out of fear, or any number of reasons. Your job is to move them away from that culture.

Talk to the police. If your teen is in a gang that means the gang is in your neighbourhood or local school. Talk to neighbours, talk to the head teacher, talk to the council. Become an activist to try and stamp out the gang in your community. It could help save your teen's life.

If there's A Gang In the Neighbourhood

Gangs operate everywhere. You might find more of them in inner city areas, but they're not isolated there, by any means. How do you know if there's a gang in your community? Increased graffiti and tagging on walls can be a good indicator, along with an increase in street crime. Just because teens hang around somewhere, though, don't automatically assume they're a gang; in the majority of instances, they won't be, they'll simply be kids talking and having fun.

If you suspect there is a gang, ask your teen. They'll know. If one exists, talk to the police, and ask for increased patrols. Talk to shopkeepers in the community, community leaders, teachers, and those in the neighbourhood watch. If everyone works together, you can eliminate the gang problem in your neighbourhood, which will keep your own teen a lot safer.

Chapter 20

Clothing

Teens often use their wardrobe as an extension of their personalities, so like teens themselves their clothes can be provoking, frustrating and even completely surprising to their parents. However, parents are often the source of funding for these clothes and if they have household rules regarding wardrobe choices then these regulations should be discussed openly. Parents should also strive to understand the trends that their teens conform to, as popular culture often provides another set of rules that a teen's wardrobe tends to follow.
Household Rules Regarding Teen Wardrobes
Just about every parent feels differently about their teen's chosen wardrobe. Before setting down any hard household rules regarding teen clothes, parents should consider a few pertinent questions. To begin with, how much clothing does your teen need? If (s)he regularly wears a uniform to school then the amount of clothing that (s)he has control over is considerably lessened. If, however, (s)he needs to work every day or requires special outfits for a certain activity then his or her wardrobe will likely become more extensive. Next, what type of clothing does your teen need? If (s)he must look presentable then it is likely that (s)he will need both more dressy as well as more casual clothing. Also think about the condition of the clothes you would like your teen to wear. If you won't tolerate ripped, stained or wrinkled clothes then you need to have on hand solutions for how to deal with these problems when they do occur. Finally, consider the image that you would like your teen to project. If short skirts and tops, slouchy pants, and/or clothing with inappropriate messages or designs are not acceptable to you then you need to make sure that your teen knows this.

Understanding Popular Trends

As parents you'll need to take off the rose coloured glasses and understand that regardless of your household rules most teens would rather conform to the popular trends than your wishes when it comes to their wardrobes. One way to mitigate the arguments that could arise is to stay current with popular trends. Understanding how, and why, teens want to dress the way they do will not only give you great insight into your teen's preferences but also his or her personality. It may also allow you to find a common middle ground that accommodates your teen's wishes as well as your own desires when it comes to setting household teen clothing rules.

Dealing With Delicates

Most arguments regarding teen wardrobes centre around the clothing that can be seen by others, but don't forget that you may need to address your teen's underclothing as well. It can be hard to talk about "unmentionables" with teens, so taking a matter of fact attitude might be helpful. For example, asking your son if he prefers boxers and briefs and in which size will net you all the information you need to know for buying his underwear in the future. Similarly, if you feel it is time for your daughter to be fitted for a bra then taking her to a store in which the saleswomen can confidently measure her will help lend a professional air that will help lessen any embarrassment. Every now and then checking in if your child needs new underwear will help you know that (s)he has a good foundation for his or her wardrobe.

Teen wardrobes can be an inflammatory topic, one that can cause passionate disagreements between teens and their parents. By setting a few house rules, staying current on teen trends and making sure that your teen has appropriate undergarments parents can help defuse these disagreements and restore a degree of calm regarding their teens clothes.

Chapter 29

Encourage Platonic Friendships

Very often teenagers will suddenly feel strange around their friends of the opposite sex, even if they have lived next to each other for years or used to spend hours at a time catching bugs/playing football/building forts in the back garden. As parents it can be hard to see this awkwardness develop, particularly when the friendship had previously been a strong and supportive one. Rather that passively allow your teen to drift apart from good friends, actively encourage him or her to maintain platonic friendships. If (s)he seems hesitant, discuss the many benefits of such friendships and see if there is anything that you can do to help the friendship flourish.

As a parent you might think that your input is not wanted when it comes to your teen's friendships and this may be true, but it doesn't mean that it's not needed. Teens tend to be hyperconscious of what others think and this can obscure the bigger reality of a situation. For example, if none of their friends have platonic friendships then they are unlikely to remain best friends with someone of the opposite sex – even if it means foregoing a great friendship for no good reason. If you feel that your teen is caught in such a trap, casually ask about his or her most cherished platonic friendships. Even saying something as simple as "I bet Mary would like to go see that film" or "You should loan that book to John, he'd probably love it" may be enough to remind your teen of his or her friends. Such pointed hints also give teens an easy way out: if anyone questions them about interacting with a friend of the opposite sex then they can always say that you asked them to do it.

Discuss the Benefits of Platonic Friendships
If you've been making casual comments about a platonic friendship and your teen just doesn't seem to be biting you may need to sit down with him or her and have an obvious discussion about the benefits of platonic friendships. Remind your teen that staying friendly with members of the opposite sex will give them an insight into how the other gender works including how they think, what they find interesting, what they consider important and what they definitely don't consider important. A lot of these things might be a big surprise to your teen! Also, having a friend who is a member of the opposite sex means that your teen will have an opportunity to hear advice and opinions that none of his or her other friends may be able to give him or her. Finally, if nothing else works, remind your teen that a friend of the opposite sex also has a lot more friends of that sex…

Ask if There is Anything You Can Do
Your teen may not always ask you for advice when (s)he needs help, so go ahead and jump the gun – ask your teen if there is anything that you can do to help him or her maintain a platonic relationship. You may be rewarded with a shrug, but you just might find that is something simple that you can do that (s)he has built up to stressful proportions in his or her mind. Be patient because this may be a hard conversation for your teen, and always remind him or her that you just want what's best and makes them happy. If you say it enough your teen just might begin to believe it!

Chapter 30

Teenage Sleep Patterns

It's as if it's programmed into them. As they become teenagers, suddenly kids are staying up later, usually a lot later, and don't want to get up in the morning. Give them half a chance and they'll sleep in until ten or noon. That can be annoying on a school morning, and upset your whole household routine. It's as if their whole system has gone out of kilter.

In fact, according to research, that's exactly what happens. Instead of producing melatonin around 10 pm, like most of us, teenagers don't produce it until 1 am, meaning they're awake and alter much later. That's why it can be almost impossible to prise them away from the computer, video game console or TV at night. Whether it's all due to behaviour or hormonal, no one knows yet, but it exists.

They still need sleep, of course – in fact they need more of it than either adults or children for their growth – but going to bed later means they do actually need to sleep later. So dragging them up at eight on the weekend when they haven't fallen asleep until one or two is, in fact, a bad thing. Medically, the best thing you can do is simply let them rest. Of course, that's not possible on days when they have to go to school or work. They have to be up, and that means, in many cases, you have to get them up. It's frustrating, and simply insisting that they go to bed earlier isn't going to work if they're only going to lie there awake.

Is it possible to find a compromise? Possibly. A good alarm clock will help, as well as instilling as much self-discipline in them as you can. But it's still not going to be perfect, and there will still be mornings when you'll have to drag the duvet off them and shepherd them out of the door.

Weekends

In general, weekends are a little easier (unless they have a paper round or a Saturday job, of course). You can simply let them sleep later. But it can seem galling when your teen stumbles into the living room at noon or one after you've already been up for hours. Just tell yourself that they really need the sleep, and possibly set a limit – they have to be up by noon at the latest, for instance.

Curfews

Many teens are very social. They're out with friends at night, sometimes very late indeed, and you find yourself lying awake, worrying, and listening for the sound of the key in the lock.

Going out is fine on the weekends, when they don't have to be up early the next morning. But with many teens, certainly up to the age of 17, you should have times by which they need to be home. Sit down and discuss these with them. Give your reasons for picking a certain hour and listen to their inevitable arguments against them. Allow them to be later with notification (they have mobiles, they can call) and a very good excuse, as long as it's a rare occurrence. But make it clear that breaking curfew without that will result in being punished. After the first time it happens, they'll believe you! Make a good distinction between weekdays and weekends.

The next time it's noon and you go up to wake them, try to remember that they were once your little angels – it helps!

Chapter 31

Getting Their First Job

Teens have a lot to think about when they contemplate finding their first job and putting together a good CV (curriculum vitae) is just one facet of an employment search. A CV, sometimes also referred to as a resume, helps a teen list out their personal contact information, skills and experiences that would be pertinent for a new job as well as provide information regarding referees who are happy to give them a recommendation. However, just because parents have written CVs before does not mean that they should take over and do the CV writing for their teens as well. Instead, parents should direct teens toward resources that will help them write their own CVs and then remain available to offer guidance while their teens work through the CV writing on their own.

Teens and Curriculum Vitae (CV) Writing

Teens who have never attempted to put together a resume or CV will likely have no idea where to start. It is a parent's job to help guide them towards a template or another example that will help them explore the pertinent sections of a good CV. For example, parents may wish to share a version of their own CV, help teens find a good website explaining how to write a CV or even invest in a reference book on CV and other business writing. Very often school and public libraries offer such resources, so a quick trip prior to the day of CV writing could be a good idea for parents and teens.

Pertinent Sections of a Teen CV

A teen CV will obviously be shorter than an adult CV but that does not mean that it should not contain the same pertinent sections. All CVs should start with the contact details of the job candidate, including name, telephone number, mailing address and email address, and then include sections on education to date and any relevant work experience. If a teen has no formal work experience then listing voluntary experiences may be appropriate instead. If a teen has any exceptional skills then including a miscellaneous skills section may be a good idea as well. Finally, CVs should end with the contact details of two referees that are not related to the teen. These referees should have already agreed to speak on behalf of the teen, and only the contact details that they have agreed to should be shared with potential employers.

Helping a Teen Prepare a CV

Teens can often work well from a good template, but parents should also remain available to help their teens prepare their first CVs. Providing teens with a computer, printer and paper, offering to proofread their drafts, helping teens brainstorm about key phrases or skills and reminding teens to double check listed information and spelling are all ways that parents can help a teen prepare a CV. If a teen has a particular job in mind, then parents can also help angle the CV towards this particular form of employment to help teens maximise their chances of a successful job application.

Preparing a teen CV can be a nerve-wracking experience, but it is one that teens do need to work through with some degree of independence. While parents can help teens with CV writing by organising appropriate resources, pinpointing pertinent sections of the document and remaining available to help throughout the process, parents should not take over and write the CV themselves. Instead, parents and teens can use this time to work together to help make a teen's first job search successful.

It might be that your teen leaves school, either at 16 or 18, and has trouble finding a job. That's certainly not uncommon these days for those with no or low qualifications. It can be a very frustrating time, especially if their friends are working and earning money. All they have to fill their time is TV during the day, which is hardly inspiring viewing. When they do see their friends at night, they have next to no money to spend, too.

As a parent, you hurt for them in the situation. They want to work, but what can you do to help them?

Practical Help

The obvious place to send them is the Job centre. That, along with the Connexions agency, can put them in touch with employers in the area who might be able to use them. Of course, it's no guarantee of a job, but at least it can put them on the right road. More than that, it makes them feel as if they're doing something to find work. There might be a number of disappointments along the way, but every step brings them closer.

Make sure they have the best possible CV. It really can make a difference. Well laid out and printed, it can tip the scales in your teen's favour. Also, if they appear well-dressed for an interview, looking eager, that will help them tremendously. They might say it's not necessary, but try to make sure they put on their best clothes for an interview and go in well-groomed.

Since money will be an issue for them, ensure they receive all the benefits they can, which will essentially be Jobseekers' Allowance. It's not a lot, but it's better than them having nothing in their pocket. Be understanding about finances, don't charge them rent - they can pay once they're working - and if they need a little extra from time to time, slip it to them if you can afford it. Their gratitude will be worthwhile.

If their strategies for finding a job aren't working, sit down with them, analyse what they've been doing, and help them come up with new ideas. Be a part of the team, on their side, and work with them to make it happen. After all, you're the one with experience. Share it and pass it on.

Emotional Support
Emotional support is vital if they're having difficulty finding a job. Inevitably, after a while, possibly a very short while, they'll feel discouraged. You need to be there to reassure them that they will find work, and give them a push when they need it, at those times when they might find it hard to motivate themselves.
Try not to let them become too down about the situation. Take them out for a meal and cheer them up. Contact friends to see if they know of anything. Investigate home-based businesses they might be able to run and gain some income, even if it's only part-time. All the positive steps you can take help them - and who knows, a business from home might turn into a good money-maker.
In fact, if they have business ideas take them seriously and investigate the feasibility of putting them into action. Some can be achieved for little investment, and there are also agencies willing to help the young set up their own business. Your teen might turn out to be the next Richard Branson!
But one of the greatest things you can do for your teen in the long-term, especially if they're having difficulty find a job, is encouraging them to go to college and gain qualifications that will help finding work in the future much easier.

Chapter 32

How to Get Your Teen to Talk

It can be easier said then done to encourage your teenager to talk, but here are some practical ideas to help you.

Ask For Their Opinion – to help open up a teen into talking, try asking for their opinion in conversation. Don't despair if their answer is controversial though, as this could be another teen shock tactic in action.

Talk To Their Friends – when they've got friends around, be friendly and chatty (but not overpowering) to their friends, as this may bring out a desire in your teen to chat to you as well. It helps if their friends think you're cool.

Chat Via Email, IM or Text – it sounds extreme, but if your teen really isn't up for chatting much face-to-face, then why not resort to the methods they use for communication. Three key ways are chatting via text, instant messaging or email.

Corner Them – if things are getting really bad on the communication side of things, then you may have to resort to cornering your teen. Catch them when they come home from school or college, or at a mealtime, and try and engage them in conversation.

Make Time for Chat at Mealtimes – many families no longer sit down for family meals together, but this is a great tradition to have an a good opportunity to talk to each other. If it doesn't fit in with plans every day, then try and set aside days each week when you can make time.

Ask a Sibling or Other Relative to Talk to Them – if your teen is uncommunicative with you, perhaps it may help to ask an older sibling, cousin or other relative to chat to them for you? It may help to emphasise the fact that you, the parent, are not trying to interfere or be bossy, but would like to know they're okay and chat sometimes.

Be There to Talk When Your Teen Wants To – if your teenager seems to be resisting all attempts to chat most of the time, then do let them know that you're there to chat to them whenever they want to. They may feel they can't talk to you, or that you've not got time for them, but always let them know you have and that they can talk to you whenever they feel the need.

Above all, give them time. They will, hopefully, talk to you when they want to – and probably on their own terms, too!

Chapter 33

Becoming Independent

One thing in life that you can't stop is your teens growing. Yes, part of that means them growing away from you, but it's inevitable, it's the way of becoming an adult. It might hurt to see it happen after looking after and nurturing them for so long, but just as they need to find themselves, so also do you need to let them go.

Obviously it doesn't happen overnight. But from the age of around 13, in small steps, help them to become gradually more independent. That way, when they do finally leave, it won't seem so bad for you – or them – and along the way you'll have a teen that's becoming more confident about themselves and about life.

Practical Measures
From the age of 14, is there any reason your teens can't wash their own clothes? Of course not, although they'll imagine there are, and you almost certainly won't catch them ironing, particularly boys. But you'll be doing them a favour if you

give them responsibility for more things surrounding their appearance.

Similarly, instead of going shopping for clothes with them, give them the money to go and do it themselves – with the possible exception of school uniforms. You might not like some of what they buy, but that's part of the process, and you'll know that everything is completely their choice.

The same applies to haircuts, or even a lack of them. Once they're old enough, let the decisions be their, not yours. What they think looks good and what you think looks good will probably be two different things, but let them express themselves as individuals.

When they're 17, encourage them to take driving lessons, even if it means you paying for them. Having a driving licence will certainly make them feel more adult, having passed a major milestone away from childhood and dependence. It might also eventually become a factor in them landing a job, and is a passport to the freedom of the road (although insurance is going to be high).

Above all, give them more privacy. Let their room be their sanctuary. Don't go in without knocking and receiving an answer. Let them feel they have a place where they can retreat away from everyone, including you. Allow them to decorate it as they wish, even if it's not to your taste. It's their space, and makes them feel it belongs to them, not you.

Emotional Growth

Although most of the elements of their personalities will be in place before they become teens, the adolescent years are when they really assert themselves as individuals. They're rapidly on the way to adulthood, so treat them that way. Include them in more adult discussions, anything from politics to the price of petrol, and listen to what they have to say. Don't belittle their opinions.

There will be tough times for them along the road, that's the nature of growth, so be willing to offer support to them. When they want to discuss something, make the time to do it, and really pay attention. It can take a lot for them to open up, so value it when they do.

When they do things or take stances you don't agree with, keep quiet. Let them try on those different clothes of attitude and behaviour, as long as they stay within the boundaries you've set. Give them room to roam. You might fear losing them, but if you give them their head, they'll come back to you when they're ready.

Make them feel secure at home, that it's a place they can always return to and feel safe. Simply loving and supporting them can do that.

Chapter 34

Leaving Home

It's a traumatic time when your teens leave home, flying the nest. Traumatic for you, that is; they're bursting to go and have their freedom for the first time. But you know that underneath there's an element of sadness to it all, and that this will always be home to them, no matter how far or how long they're gone. However, that can seem like small consolation at the time.

Some, such as those going to university, will be back soon enough, if only for a little while. For others there will only be occasional visits in the future.

Preparing Your Teen to Leave
There are many reasons for leaving, but once out of your house, your teen will need to be more self-sufficient. You'll help your own peace of mind, and well as giving them a

substantial start, if you teach them the basic skills of cooking, cleaning, sewing, how to wash their clothes – the survival skills they'll require once they're out on their own.

It's doesn't have to be an advanced course, just enough so you'll know they can fend for themselves. You won't worry, and they'll be much happier. It won't stop panicked phone calls when they try something and it goes wrong, but you'll enjoy those anyway it's an indication they're not completely grown yet.

You can prepare them for their new life materially, too. If they're moving into a flat, say, make sure it's stocked with food, pots and pans, dishes and cleaning supplies. If you give them the money to do it themselves, there will be no guarantee they'll actually buy everything, and besides, you have the experience to know what works well and what doesn't.

For those going to university halls of residence, there isn't as much to do. Just make sure everything is in place financially – and drive them down there to help deliver all their stuff (it also means you can take a look at the place).

Without Your Teen Around

You might have been dreaming of the moment when your teen leaves for years. But when it happens the house will seem very empty. Of course, there might be younger kids still at home, so everyone will feel a mix of loneliness and more space.

However much you miss them, you need to give your teen time to adjust to a new life. They have a lot of exploring to do, so give them the room to do it. Limit the calls to once a week, and only go to see their new place when they issue an invitation (of course, if it's not been forthcoming after a while, you'd be perfectly fair in making the suggestion yourself).

At the same time, make it perfectly clear that they're welcome at home any time, whether it's for a cup of tea, Sunday lunch, or to stay an entire weekend. Issue invitations – not all the time, but often enough so they know you mean it – without being insistent. You'll be surprised; even the hardest of them will be homesick from time to time.

Once they've had a chance to discover themselves, you'll probably find they become regular visitors, if only to have their washing done properly and to have a good, filling meal.

About the author

Damon as spent a lot of time and done some intensive research to put this handbook for parents with teenagers together searching the internet, reading parenting books for the best up to date information on Children and Teenagers. Putting all the information he had found together for you in this one informative handbook for you to use with your children and teenagers.

Damon is one of the UK's leading professional Teenage Behavioural Therapist's and has over 13 years experience of working with hard to engage teenagers as a Behavioural Therapist, Mentor and as a Mediator.
He is a male counsellor/psychotherapist who has his own private practice and is an Integrative Practitioner which means he blends different methods of counselling according to the individual young persons needs. He has experience of working with young people and adults from different Ethnicity, Race and Cultures. He believes that his own life experiences are just as important as his professional and academic training in relating to young people.

He researched therapeutic behavioural programmes in the UK and Europe and upon discovering that none were in existence set about putting together a programme.
He started Teenbratcampuk in 2008 (www.teenbratcampuk.co.uk) which is a therapy programme for young people based in an outdoor setting. It is a therapeutic programme for troubled teenagers which he personally facilitates and also counsels.

The intent and purpose of the Troubled Teen Therapy Programme (TTTP) is to provide an impacting, therapeutic experience for behavioural issues.

It offers sustainable solutions to families struggling to manage young people (11-18 years old) with behavioural problems. Too often, traditional approaches for addressing antisocial behaviour and substance use have failed to substantiate their effectiveness to reduce or correct undesirable behaviours. The TTTP model can be effective in reducing antisocial behaviour amongst young people. The approach looks at individuals as a part of a complex network that includes the individual, their family and other outside factors including their school and peers. TTTP looks to identify to promote behaviour change in the young people in a natural environment, using existing strengths within each system (e.g. family, peers, school, neighbourhood, informal support network) to make that change.

The goal of TTTP is to enable parents with the skills and resources needed to independently address the difficulties that arise in raising teenagers and to empower the young people to cope with family, peer, school, and neighbourhood problems by equipping them with an "emotional toolbox". This enables them to deal with their issues and behaviour in a more positive way. TTTP can be effective in reducing antisocial behaviour among diverse populations of young people with high and complex needs.

TTTP can be effective with both male and female young people (and their families) of different ages, economic status and cultural backgrounds. Whilst TTTP has been shown it can be an effective treatment for diverse populations of young people, it is not a *__silver bullet__* and is therefore not appropriate for all young people. Therefore it is important to clarify which young people are appropriate and are willing to engage and change and therefore would benefit from our programmes at the application stage. TTTP targets those young people with behaviour problems that are often a result of difficulties, substance use, and multiple families, school and peer problems.

Teenbratcampuk offer an effective way of reaching defiant teens that have been hostile to parental efforts to change their behaviour.

Your young person (13-18) will be in a safe yet challenging environment where the power of the natural world combined with the professional expertise of our therapist creates a uniquely powerful and transformational experience.

We believe all young people have an inner desire to succeed and make their families proud. Sometimes years of struggle at school and with parents and teachers has made these young people turn inward. As a parent, you have probably experienced incredible frustration as you try to reason with your young person. You are fed up with the hostility and can't understand why your young person doesn't realise that all you want is for them to be HAPPY and SUCCESSFUL in life.

Young people often referred to as troubled teens, which are displaying emotional or behavioural challenges such as depression, anger/aggression, school failure, or substance abuse, are ideal candidates for our 7 day therapy programmes. This is a positive growth experience where young people are encouraged, challenged and give every opportunity to succeed.

By removing the young people from their environment, family and peers, the outdoors is used as a non-judgmental arena in which young people can challenge themselves physically and emotionally while exploring the self-defeating, reckless or self-destructive behaviours and choices from their past. The outdoors becomes a tool which quickly and effectively impacts young people.

As our trained counsellor works with the young people to help them recognise the long-term value of their experiences, young people begin to learn to accept responsibility for their actions, and to better understand the correlation between cause and effect, action and reaction.

TEENBRATCAMPUK
Troubled Teen Behavioural Programme
Welcome to Teenbratcampuk we have helped troubled teens and their families for almost 5 years. Teenbratcampuk is a therapeutic programme for troubled teens ages 11-18. We are the only provider of outdoor teen behavioural therapy programmes outside of America. Teenbratcampuk *is not* a boot camp, adventure camp, or any other kind of activity holiday camp.
Started in 2008 by our founder after identifying a lack of help and support for parents with troubled teen's. He had to think outside the box and adapted the techniques of the standard counselling protocol to develop a more flexible and creative approach, being as flexible as is necessary for each young person. Our behaviourist understands how to use the environment as a lever and a clinical tool and works outdoors with individuals and small groups of young people (minimum 1 and up to a maximum of 4) on any one programme. Regardless of the challenges, he has now been able to use his techniques to successfully work with a range of difficulties and issues with young people. All our private and exclusive programmes are run by one of the UK's leading professional Teenage Behaviourists BA (Hons) DipCoun. MBACP. CCYP. AIP sometimes with the assistance of his wife and /or

a volunteer. Our goal is to help you find solutions to the struggles you face at home with your troubled teen.

Our programmes are specifically designed to take your young person out of their comfort zone by removing them from all the things they take for granted at home. It involves camping in and around Snowdonia we give them sole responsibility for their own tent, food and cooking equipment. It is designed so that they will appreciate the comforts and privileges of their own home.

The young person will be responsible for their own tent and they will be shown the correct way to erect the tent and secure it. If they chose not to do this correctly once shown then the consequences are that only THEY may get wet and have a very uncomfortable nights sleep. They will need to collect wood every day in order to cook food and start a fire to provide warmth. Our behavioural programmes run throughout the year and are tailored to address the individual's behaviour. Our diet is basic, bland, and nutritionally sound.

The programme is for those:-

Who show NO respect for siblings, friends or family and have a very lazy/selfish attitude.

Show no consideration for others as long as they get what they want and lie constantly.

Young people struggling with emotional, addiction, and behavioural problems

An effective, intensive intervention that uses traditional therapies in an alternative setting

A short-term, high-impact experience that serves as a catalyst for positive change.

A transformational experience that helps young people to learn new behavioural skills and develop healthy self-esteem through character development.

Young people often referred to as troubled teens, which are displaying behavioural challenges such as anger/aggression, school failure, or substance abuse, are ideal candidates for our behavioural programme. This is a positive growth experience where young people are encouraged and challenged from the start. Our model of teen help is based on respect, actions/re-actions, trust, boundaries and taking responsibility for themselves.

By removing the young people from their environment, family and peers, the outdoors is used as a non-judgmental arena in which young people can challenge themselves physically and emotionally while exploring the self-defeating, reckless or self-destructive behaviours.

As our trained behaviourist works with the young people to help them recognise the long-term value of their experiences, young people begin to learn to accept responsibility for their actions, and to better understand the correlation between cause and effect, action and reaction.

Our behaviourist feels that attending one of our programmes should not be seen as a punishment, but as an opportunity for your young person to be away from family and friends for a short period and to be with people who are there to listen, support ,work with them and (if needed) to challenge them. This is to help them deal with the things that are causing their behavioural problems in a more positive and constructive way so that both they and their family can move forward. Where it has come to the point that their behaviour is on longer acceptable then things need to change for all your benefit. Teenbratcampuk runs programmes for young people in the outdoors. The programmes are very effective at changing troubled teens' behaviour and have been proven to show long-term results. Troubled youth can experience powerful personal growth on our structured programme with our therapists. Young people on our programmes are NOT yelled at, physically disciplined or ever put in any harm or unsafe position.

By taking troubled young people out of their normal environments and out of their comfort zone, they have the time to look at and talk about their behaviours and choices and start to learn from them. We use natural and logical structure, flexible and creative approach with therapy and the power of the outdoors.

Our programme fosters compliance through an experiential learning process of success. In other words, if a student does not put their tent up right on a cloudy night, he or she may get rained on and be wet all night. The students learn from experience, not fear and intimidation.

At Teenbratcampuk, the counsellors eat the same food, sleep in the same environment, and experience the same joys and misfortunes the outdoors has to offer 24 hours a day. Because the counsellor is on the same level, the students learn to admire and respect them. Ultimately, they develop very close relationships of trust and a willingness to discuss problems and issues.

Teenbratcampuk offer an effective way of reaching defiant teens that have been hostile to parental efforts to change their behaviour.

Your young person (11-18) will be in a safe yet challenging environment with the professional expertise of our behavioural therapist.

7984825R00127

Printed in Great Britain
by Amazon.co.uk, Ltd.,
Marston Gate.